About the Author

STACEY ABRAMS is an author, a serial entrepreneur, a nonprofit CEO, and a political leader. After eleven years in the Georgia House of Representatives, seven as Minority Leader, Abrams became the 2018 Democratic nominee for governor of Georgia, where she won more votes than any other Democrat in the state's history. She has founded multiple organizations devoted to voting rights, training and hiring young people of color, and tackling social issues at both the state and national levels, and she is a lifetime member of the Council on Foreign Relations. Abrams is the 2012 recipient of the John F. Kennedy New Frontier Award and the first black woman to become the gubernatorial nominee for a major party in the United States.

Praise for *Lead from the Outside*

"Abrams's own grit, coupled with her descriptions of much stumbling and self-doubt, will make [*Lead from the Outside*] touch you in a way few books by politicians can. In fact, the last one to manage it—biracial, the child of divorce, raised with little money by a single mother—became our forty-forth president."
—*The New York Times Book Review*

"Stacey Abrams writes about her personal cocktail of grit and gumption." —*Glamour*

"Stacey didn't write [*Lead from the Outside*] simply to help people in the minority; she wrote it because she believes people in the minority can help us all." —*Teen Vogue*

"Stacey Abrams has everything you want in a candidate: a good legal mind, experience in governance, and a deep knowledge of poverty and hard work. If you read [*Lead from the Outside*], you will discover she also has the superpowers of inspiring trust and knowing how to organize. You will have her as a friend, and you will want her as a governor." —Gloria Steinem

"[*Lead from the Outside*] is a special book with a special mission: to push ALL people to know that their greatness and worthiness is a birthright. Stacey's story is not just uplifting, but instructional as well. I am part of a long line of people who have admired Stacey for a long time. Read this book, and you will understand why." —Wes Moore, bestselling author of
The Other Wes Moore and *The Work*,
CEO of Robin Hood

"Stacey Abrams displays competence, confidence, and compassion in her assessment of the attributes and actions needed to deliver impact in today's complicated world. Her commentary is as real as her commitment is remarkable. [*Lead from the Outside*] is both a motivational and a mechanical manual, offering an intense focus on opportunities and an unyielding path to mitigate obstacles. I enthusiastically commend this book as a resource for those who want to grow personally and professionally, as well as for those who seek to help guide that same growth."

—Lisa M. Borders, former WNBA president, president and CEO of Time's Up

"Stacey understands what it is like to try and balance the everyday obligations of work and family, and [*Lead from the Outside*] offers a practical guide to pursuing meaningful work while acknowledging the myths of 'juggling it all.' All kinds of people face these challenges, but it can be more acute for women, people of color, members of the LGBTQ community, and others with 'outsider' status. This book is for anyone who has faced challenges while pursuing their passion, and it helps people left out of traditional ladders to success build one for themselves."

—Sherilyn Wright, assistant to the international president of International Brotherhood of Electrical Workers

"Here, [Stacey Abrams] shows readers from any marginalized population how to become their own advocates, proactively using their otherness while recognizing their fears. Not just local appeal; there are audiences out there that could really, really benefit from this book."

—*Library Journal*

Lead from the Outside

HOW TO BUILD YOUR FUTURE AND MAKE REAL CHANGE

STACEY ABRAMS

PICADOR   HENRY HOLT AND COMPANY   NEW YORK

For Mom and Dad, Andrea, Leslie, Richard,
Walter, and Jeanine, Jorden, Faith, Cameron, Riyan,
Ayren, Devin, Brandon, and Nakia

Designed by Kelly S. Too

The Library of Congress has cataloged the Henry Holt edition as follows:

Names: Abrams, Stacey, author.
Title: Minority leader : how to lead from the outside and make real change / Stacey
Abrams.
Description: First edition. | New York, New York : Henry Holt and Company, 2018. |
Includes index.
Identifiers: LCCN 2017058438 | ISBN 9781250191298 (hardcover) | ISBN 9781250191304
(ebook)
Subjects: LCSH: Abrams, Stacey, author. | African American women politicians—
Georgia—Biography. | Political participation. | Political leadership. | Social action. |
Social change. | Politicians—Georgia—Biography. | Legislators—Georgia—Biography. |
African American legislators—Georgia—Biography.
Classification: LCC E185.93.G4 A27 2018 | DDC 328.73'092 B—dc23
LC record available at https://lccn.loc.gov/2017058438

Picador Paperback ISBN 978-1-250-21480-5

First published by Henry Holt and Company, LLC, under the title *Minority Leader*

First Picador Edition: March 2019

10 9 8 7 6

When I dare to be powerful, to use my strength in the service of my vision, then it becomes less and less important whether I am afraid. —*Audre Lord*

CONTENTS

Preface to the Paperback Edition   xi

Introduction   xix

One   Dare to Want More   1

Two   Fear and Otherness   29

Three   Hacking and Owning Opportunity   53

Four   The Myth of Mentors   79

Five   Money Matters   103

Six   Prepare to Win and Embrace the Fail   131

Seven   Making What You Have Work   151

Eight   Work-Life Jenga   175

Nine   Taking Power   199

Acknowledgments   209

Index   219

PREFACE TO THE PAPERBACK EDITION

On November 16, 2018, I officially ended my bid to become the next governor of Georgia. Although Election Day was November 6, we'd gone into overtime due to the closeness of the vote and irregularities in the process. Folks were already grumbling because I had broken with political tradition in a late election-night speech, demanding a continuation of the process of counting votes. I had the temerity to refuse to meekly accept the results without question. Because that's what protocol demanded. But my life—and this book—are about knowing the rules and then deciding if they apply. Or if we need to write our own rules.

When I first wrote *Lead from the Outside*, I was a few months into my campaign. Each day as I typed out chapters, I did so between calling donors, delivering speeches, knocking on doors. I did so knowing that in the process, I created an early chronicle of what would be the hardest challenge in my life. Georgia voters had not elected a Democrat to statewide office in more than fifteen years; and the last time the state gave its electoral votes to a Democratic nominee for president was 1992. No woman or person of color had ever made the general election ballot as the gubernatorial candidate. The campaign I envisioned had been crafted out of years of experiences as a legislator, an entrepreneur and a civic activist, all of which would be called into question.

In my calculus, the scrutiny was a small price to pay. Our next governor had the potential to make an immediate, meaningful impact on people's lives. As I told my team, if we begin by believing every vote matters and always demand that our leaders work for us, then we can expand what is possible in Georgia and, by extension, across the South. A good government should be a tool that helps where it can and gets out of the way when it should. It must work for everyone, protect our investments, and defend the civil rights of all.

From my time as minority leader, winning the job during the last redistricting period, I knew the next governor would also have the power to veto maps and set our political landscape for decades to come. Georgia has a fast-growing, ethnically diverse population and, by 2026 or so, will be the first majority-minority state in the Deep South. As governor, I could ensure our state maps accurately represent the diversity of the state and give a voice to every community.

My victory would also be a historic one: the election of the first black woman to serve as a governor in the United States. Almost daily, I parried questions about the significance and symbolism of my bid. What did my run signal for people of color, for women, for a new generation of leaders, for women of color? My answer evolved over time, but the core remained the same: I had an obligation to build a coalition of voters who reflected the diversity of our state, our nation. I would run a campaign that began with growing the civic power of Georgians, a power I would ask them to use to help me lead the state. Simply by winning, I would redefine our belief in what leadership looks like.

In May 2018, I became the first black woman to receive the gubernatorial nomination of a major party in American history. On November 6, 2018, I received more votes than any Democrat in Georgia history, outpacing President Barack Obama and Secretary of State Hillary Clinton. I learned later that our campaign tripled the turnout of Latinos and Asian Americans, more than doubled the youth participation rate. I received more votes from African Americans than the *sum total* of Democratic voters in 2014. My candidacy created a path to win a congressional seat and flip sixteen legislative seats. I received the highest percentage of the white vote recorded in a generation. And I was within 1.4 percent of the man who had run the election and run against me—serving as both contestant and referee.

So, on the night of November 16, I returned to my initial mission and to the thousands of people I'd met along the campaign trail. Though cliché, nothing is more profound in the act of running for office than actually *talking* to voters, especially those people who are too often left out of the conversation about the future. When called upon to accept that the results of the vote would not give me the victory, I accepted the math. But when told to perform the traditional dance of concession, I vigorously declined. While I knew that, according to the law, I had to tell my fellow Georgians that our jointly imagined future would be delayed, I refused to play my scripted part. Because the game had been rigged. Again.

This analysis isn't new, nor is it news. For those of us on the outside, the quest for power is always rigged. Sometimes it's because we don't know how to gain entry, or because the winners

get to play by a different set of rules. In elections, our nation
has fought a lifelong battle about who gets to have a say in the
outcome—and set the terms of the next battle. Race, gender, and
class have been constant markers of access, beginning with the
Constitution. My election was no different. Poor communities
found themselves without equipment for voting, including missing power cords and antiquated machines. Other voters arrived
at their polling stations only to be turned away because they'd
been illegally purged or because the poll workers didn't have
enough paper for extra ballots. Some stood in hours-long lines,
while their compatriots had to give up and go back to work or
risk a family's already meager paycheck. This is how the game of
elections gets rigged.

In my non-concession speech, most political folks expected
me to turn a blind eye to the complaints and the outcome. They
were looking for me to say that no compromise of our democracy had occurred, and most expected polite compromise in the
language I used to call an end to the fight. But, unfortunately for
them, I'd read my book. And I understand conceding the election would not be right. I admit the playing field is never level, and
the reality is that a number of us enjoy a degree of privilege over
another at various points. Yet, knowing a truth does not make it
correct. Right and wrong remain valid, real constructs, and the
2018 Georgia elections crossed the line. And I said so. On national
television.

I held myself accountable, as leaders must, even when the
result would be snide comments, angry op-eds and unreturned
calls from former friends. This was a question of right and wrong.
What's not right is giving credence to bad actions, and thereby
becoming complicit. That was true on November 16, and it will
be the crucible for each challenge I will face in my life—and every

challenge you will face in yours. There is right and there is wrong, and it's important to distinguish between the two in every choice, in every hard moment of decision. Do we concede, do we compromise, or do we fight? These are the options.

Concession accepts an act as right or proper. And society's existence necessitates the act of compromise—of bending our wants to the needs of others. Leadership is a constant search for the distinction between when compromise is an act of power and when concession masks submission—or when the fight is on. I know this election demanded a moment to be uncompromising—to build a future without conceding my principles. I refused to be gaslighted into throwing away my power, diminishing my voice. Because I don't simply speak for myself. I had the hopes, dreams and demands of 1.9 million Georgians standing with me. And thousands more who had been unfairly, unlawfully silenced. And whether speaking up is about an unfair election or a flawed system of workplace promotion, the obligation remains the same: once we recognize that wrong exists, we must fight to change it every day.

When I first wrote *Lead from the Outside*, I wanted to deconstruct the successes and failures I had and distill them into potential guidelines for others. More, I wanted to rethink how we cast everyday challenges into such distinct categories. From discussing my personal debt or my brother's constant struggle for sobriety and freedom, my mission was to shake our internalization of false narratives about who is worthy of opportunity. As an intensely private person, writing this book served as a dry run for office, where every foible, decision, or gaffe would be recast into a thirty-second commercial questioning my humanity and fashion choices. Colleagues who'd known me for more than a decade had never known about my brother's incarceration, and customers of my companies learned about my business acumen and my silent ownership stakes.

I remain intensely private, but I understand the fragility of the distance I'd maintained for so long. And that is likely a good thing. In the middle of the campaign, standing in line for tea at the airport, a server from the restaurant next door charged up to me and wrapped me in a bear hug. I racked my brain to identify him, but instinctively, I returned the embrace. Turns out, we'd never met. But when the stranger let me go, he smiled broadly. "Thank you," he said gruffly. "I owe student loans and take care of my momma. Thanks for telling folks the truth. We're people too. You've got my vote."

Again and again, across the course of this marathon, Georgians of every stripe would grasp my hand, hug me, or buss my cheek, whispering their truths to me. "My daughter is just like your Walter. God and I love her, and we believe in her." "I'm broke, but I'm a good person." "I want to run, but I thought I had to wait my turn." And over and over, I realized that candor, whether in the pages of this book or on the trail, transformed stories into lived truths shared by those who would never know their common bond. When I traveled across the country, I found the same repeated—our narratives are singular but not unique.

Understanding how my story liberated others to tell their own, I understand more why I wrote this book in the first place. It's the same reason I refused to back down about how unfair our elections process has become and the danger it poses to the democratic experiment that is America. I have to speak up because silence is not only dangerous, it is corrosive. When we refuse to name our obstacles, we can never find a way around them. Worse, we accept their inevitability, believing we deserve what we get.

I also wrote this book to be the outsider's version of *The Art of War*, only this time, we're fighting for our rightful place at the table, in the boardroom, and eventually, in office. Thus, I took my own advice and turned my rage and pain into action on November 16. Not only did I refuse to concede, I created a new organization with the mission to guarantee better elections for those who follow. With my next steps, I will leverage anger into fixing what I know is broken, and in the process, show others to be resilient in their battles for the justice they seek. With the constant reminder that the battle will be hard, marked with defeats and I may never be the direct beneficiary of success.

Those who pick up this book to hate-read and find reasons to reaffirm their low opinion of me will be duly rewarded. They will read this book as a rejection of the normal order. As I said that night, I'm supposed to say nice things and accept my fate. As outsiders, we are expected to continue on as the system commands, primarily to preserve our ability to participate and, just maybe, one day, win the lottery of opportunity to be the one who slips inside the door. I fully recognize the process and how effective it is. My problem is, I don't like it, and I believe we can fix it. Not simply by dismantling what has been carefully constructed by centuries of patriarchy, racism, classism, and bigotry— no one has that kind of time. Instead, we have to hack it. Figure out its flaws, identify backdoors, and overwhelm the system. Consider this my call to arms.

When I wrote *Lead from the Outside*, I asked myself what I valued in a leader, what excited me about the work I had done across sectors and communities, and at different moments in my life. Leadership requires the ability to engage and to create empathy for communities with disparate needs and ideas, and that's why as outsiders, we can make the best and most effective leaders. Telling an effective story demands a similar skill set. Good storytelling takes the reader into a life that is both familiar and foreign, enough of both to make space for others to feel empowered to tell their stories.

I know the lessons I set out to share and the values I sought to advocate remain true—perhaps even more so. I could not have gotten through the last year of my life, through the grueling ten days after Election Day, if I didn't know what I was fighting for, waking up for, speaking out for, flying across the country for, raising money for. Greatness demands purpose—in the face of upended expectations and extreme setbacks, even more so. I have faced the toughest loss I can imagine, and I know I will lose again and again. But I will never fail to try.

INTRODUCTION

In November 1994, I entered a hotel room in Jackson, Mississippi, the dusk of late autumn broken by streetlights that flickered against the window. I'd spent the day vying for a title no one like me had ever won before, one I had no road map for winning. What I had instead were two parents, Robert and Carolyn, who sat and waited in that hotel for me, the second of their six children, while I tried.

The Rhodes Scholarship committee called the daylong session an interview, but the experience felt more like a grueling oral exam—a cross between *Jeopardy!* and Celebrity Trivial Pursuit with questions about foreign ministers, abstract painters, and dead scientists. Prior to my junior year of college, I had known little of the Rhodes, the Truman, the Marshall, or the Fulbright. These prestigious awards, I thought, were only chased by students who spent summers abroad or did postgraduate study in Europe. Fellowships like this were an unlikely topic of conversation for first-generation college students or their children. So when the Rhodes panel had asked how winning their scholarship would change my life, I stumbled. I didn't know, and even sitting there, the prize nearly within my reach, I feared learning the answer.

I had feared it so much, in fact, that I almost hadn't submitted my application. I had offered excuse after excuse to the professors who exhorted me to apply: England was too cold; the application too long; I had better things to do with my time. In truth, though, I didn't want to apply for the Rhodes Scholarship because I didn't want to lose. And I knew I wouldn't win.

I was afraid that outside the comfort of my black women's college, I would prove all those who had looked down on me correct: I was a big fish in a multiculti pond, but I couldn't compete with the true heirs to American power. The Rhodes was not for the likes of me, or those who looked like me, and certainly not for working-class kids, especially a working-class black woman. Because at twenty, I had fully internalized all the "-isms" that taught me to strive but not exceed my limits.

Plus, I had research to back this up. Only a small number of African American students had ever won the Rhodes by 1994, and no black woman had ever been the Rhodes nominee from Mississippi. But, when I finally admitted my fear to the dean of my college, I found the response I received strangely compelling. You're almost guaranteed to win, she said, if you get past Mississippi.

Hope sparked for an instant when she laid out the pathway to success. I could win this rare victory if I could outshine others from my home state. But if beating the odds in Mississippi was the only way to Britain, I wouldn't bother packing my bags. Mississippi had perfected soul-crushing poverty wrapped in gentility. The state had birthed my parents and tried mightily to deny them futures. It failed, but not for lack of trying. *Get past Mississippi.* The phrase barely captured the stark reality of the "where" that raised me.

My parents had followed the rules for advancement as they understood them: they finished high school, graduated from college. My mother, one of seven, not only defied family tradition by crossing her high school stage with a diploma, she excelled in college and went on to receive a master's degree in library science. My father, the first man in his family to go to college, did so despite an undiagnosed learning disability. They secured the degrees that should have guaranteed success.

My parents, who had marched for civil rights as teenagers, also knew intimately that the end of Jim Crow did not mean the rise of black prosperity. And they knew the advantages of education provided no security. They worked hard, did everything they were supposed to do—my mom as a librarian, my dad as a shipyard worker—and yet despite following the American prescription for prosperity, they sometimes barely kept their heads above water.

My mom never liked the descriptors of our economic status like "working class" or "working poor," so she called us the "genteel poor"—we had little money, but we read books and watched PBS. More important, our parents refused to believe that their lot meant their children could not do better than they had. Instead, they created their own prescription, known in our family as the Trinity for Success: go to church, go to school, and take care of one another.

We may not have had running water every day, and the power bill might go unpaid, but nothing interfered with my parents' trinity of education, faith, and service—service to family, service to others. Inside our house, we three older girls each had personal responsibility for a younger sibling. On Saturday mornings, my younger brother Richard would creep into my room and over to my side of the bed I shared with my sister Leslie. He would shake my shoulder until I woke, and I'd follow him groggily into the living room where the television sat mute until I pulled the knob to bring the cartoons. Richard knew to wake me because he was my charge. Our eldest sister, Andrea, cared for the baby, Jeanine, and Leslie watched over our youngest brother, Walter. Often, later on Saturdays, we would volunteer at a soup kitchen or in a youth detention center, where my parents reminded us that no matter how little we had, there was always someone with less, and it was our job to serve that person.

Our parents also taught us to learn for the sake of knowledge itself, and they made certain we understood no one could take knowledge from us. Circumstances could steal your house, your job, your car, but no one could take the contents of our minds. With learning, they believed, we could always find a way. And proof of our knowledge—a college degree—would be a tangible reminder to those who doubted us because of our skin color.

The neighborhood where we lived, comprising two streets, was working class and entirely black, at least until I was in fifth grade or so. I remember when the Brooks family moved in, the first white people to live in our area. Growing up, our sister Andrea, served as the ringleader, organizing our games and managing our recreation. We were probably the only kids in our community who played Library or voluntarily watched ballroom dancing.

Church anchored our souls, providing a steady diet of lessons for navigating the uncertainties of a life of working-class poverty. We soaked up parables from the Bible mixed with real-life stories of the men and women of the civil rights movement. Our faith, which taught us to reach beyond our mortal selves, lent gravity to what we were taught by my parents' daily lessons.

The emphasis my family placed on faith, learning, and service gained me access into Spelman College, and I had a respectable 3.65 GPA, but nothing like the 4.0s Rhodes scholars possessed. My record of community service could not be faulted, but the summer before, I'd met other potential applicants who had saved small villages in India or spoke fluent Farsi. My farthest travels had taken me to Ithaca, New York, and Scottsdale, Arizona.

Small insults had also built a layer of resistance to risk in me. Once, in middle school, after I won a citywide essay contest, my dad drove me to pick up my prize. While he waited in the car, I ran inside to receive my ribbon and my $50 reward. But the woman in charge—white and grim-faced when I introduced myself—refused to give me the money. I couldn't be the author of the winning essay, she declared to the others milling around the school lobby. When I protested, she demanded that I produce photo identification, an impossibility for an eighth grader. I demanded my prize, but inwardly granted her the validity of her doubts. Hers was not the first or last nick in my confidence. Again and again, throughout my childhood, teachers had challenged my right to be in advanced classes, to question their assumptions, to presume equal rights to my peers. Although I usually insisted on going forward, the repeated doubts took root. What if they were correct?

Even in an all-black college, I grappled with fears of inadequacy. I had once imagined becoming a physicist. I'd been a top physics student in high school, and published in a university's academic journal as a twelfth grader. My freshman year, I took an advanced course at the college across the street, where they still had seats available. I sat in the course, surrounded by men. While I was not an A student, I held my own through midterms. Shortly before an exam, the professor held me back after class. He cautioned me that I might not be suited to the complexities of higher math the long-term pursuit of physics required. A student at a women's college, I chafed at his warning, but his prediction wormed its way into my confidence.

When the next semester enrollment came around, I did not select any new physics courses. Instead, I flirted with other majors, slowly abandoning my interest in the hard sciences. If I didn't try to become a physicist, I knew I couldn't fail. Four years later, as I grappled with the Rhodes, I again balked at an opportunity because I had decided early on that I wouldn't attempt what I could not win. And my loss seemed certain—I was black and a girl and from the wrong family and the wrong zip code.

Looking back, I clearly see reality did not mirror my internal dialogue. By my senior year, I had spoken at the thirtieth anniversary of the March on Washington, been hired by the Ford Foundation to write about youth poverty, was an A student and president of the student body. But for me, each achievement felt grounded in race and class and gender. I was really good at being a black woman, when compared to other black women. But could I be more than that? My answer seemed to be a resounding "no." A small voice said I could do what I had done in that freshman physics class and concede before I tested myself. But a louder one declared I could look to my accomplishments, to the places where my otherness had been celebrated, and leverage the confidence I'd earned there. In this contest, I could use the factors of race and gender to beat the rigged system. If I could get past Mississippi, it might be my otherness that did the trick.

I relented and applied and received an invitation to come to

Jackson for the interview. The committee appeared unimpressed with my answers, and I left my interview deflated, certain that the hopes pressed into me by my parents and professors had been proven false.

I heard the results later that afternoon, standing shoulder to shoulder with the other applicants. Without the benefit of cell phones in 1994, I hurried back to the hotel where my parents waited. I walked the several blocks because I had no money for a cab. With a click of the key, I entered the hotel room and told my parents the news. The Mississippi Rhodes panel had selected me as one of their two standard-bearers to Texas for the finals. I had broken the curse: a black woman would speak for our state. And in the aftermath of my announcement, I watched my father cry.

We talked for a long time that night. About how scared I was about trying and failing, about what losing in Texas might mean. My deepest fear found voice—that I would disappoint them by not measuring up. That because of the "-isms" arrayed against my race and my gender and my background, I would never be enough. My mother told me, her throat tight, "We know what the Rhodes Scholarship is, baby. But we never imagined, from where we began, we would have a daughter who would have this opportunity. We're so proud of you. You can't fail, even if you don't win. Because you've already won the hardest part."

A few weeks later, I traveled to Texas where I did not win the Rhodes Scholarship. The loss devastated me in ways it took years to catalog; but in the attempt, I changed my life. Because I suddenly saw opportunity where I had never been brave enough to look before, and I found that failure wasn't fatal, that otherness held an extraordinary power for clarity and invention.

Armed with that loss, I would return to Texas and get a

master's degree from the University of Texas. I would attend Yale Law School, the most exclusive in the country, where I would try to confront the questions of race and gender in a space that prided itself on its meritocracy, on ignoring the value of privilege, though I could count the number of folks who looked like me in a class on one hand. When I graduated from Yale, I joined a white-shoe law firm, where I was the only person of color who practiced my type of tax law. Despite the long history of the firm, only two people of color had ever become partners—and this was one of the more diversity-conscious law firms in Atlanta.

I published romance novels and chafed at stereotypes that placed me on shelf spaces designated for urban black writers rather than in the general romantic suspense category. Between the publishers and the bookstores, they assumed a black writer with black characters couldn't appeal across color lines with her stories. So instead of sharing shelves with Nora Roberts and Elizabeth Lowell, I squeezed in between all the other women romance writers of color in our assigned section.

For every success—becoming deputy city attorney, running for office, and rising in less than four years to serve as the minority leader of the Georgia House of Representatives—I have consistently confronted racism, sexism, ageism, and other phobias about my otherness.

Still, I must work each day to silence the voices of the essay judge and the physics professor, and even my own, when I doubt what I have the potential to become. In defiance of my fears, I have launched national campaigns and won and lost elections, and I have started companies that folded and succeeded. I took the lead of a broken party, knowing that we would wander in the political wilderness for at least a decade. Then I decided to run for governor of a state in the Deep South, and in the attempt, become the first black woman to lead a state in our nation's history.

But that night in Jackson remains with me always, as a reminder that leadership is not divined by pedigree or demography and that origin stories are simply the beginning.

As a forty-four-year-old African American woman working to transform the politics of Georgia—a southern state on the brink of majority-minority status—I continue to grapple with the questions I confronted in Jackson. In my run for governor, reporters describe worries about my ability to win an election with white voters. The same question is not posed about my white opponents' ability to cultivate voters of color, although we comprise 47 percent of the population in Georgia.

My candidacy is the culmination of what I learned in pursuing the Rhodes—that what I seek to achieve is bigger than any prejudices about who I am. Call it success, leadership, confidence, or any of a dozen descriptions; what we're in pursuit of is power: the power to control our lives, to change our fates, and to win what some have been raised to take for granted. But there are few how-to guides to help those of us who are "other" to become the ones in charge. Power and leadership are hard, and it's especially difficult for those who start out weighed down by stereotypes and lack of access. Convincing others—and often ourselves—that we can overcome obstacles takes confidence, guile, and tactical maneuvers. I have learned how to seize opportunity, how to plan for victory and for defeat, and how to acquire, hold, and wield power, and I wrote this book to share what I've learned and the strategies I employed.

Leadership stands at the crux of how we get to power, and it demands the willingness to go first, to take responsibility as well as hold authority, to help others get where they need to go.

I've seen leaders emerge out of nowhere in moments of great turmoil. But more often, a leader evolves from a good person who is willing to make hard choices and handle the consequences. Effective leadership can be difficult to find in general, but for some of us, we find ourselves blocked or discouraged, confronting power we aren't supposed to have.

Almost weekly, I sit on panels and in meetings talking to women, young leaders, and people of color—those who are told they are not supposed to be in charge—about how I got to where I am and where I plan to go next. One thing comes up again and again in these discussions: that our otherness operates as disqualification, and our inherent qualities render us less than others, and therefore unworthy. In *Lead from the Outside*, I want to dispel the bigotry of that thinking, and I want to talk about how those of us who stand on the outside can charge right in.

Inevitably, wherever I speak, I get the question "How do you do it?" But I think the most important question is this one: "How do I banish doubts and get out of my own way?" The straight answer is that you must. No one born into the minority has the luxury of giving up, even if we do not win enough of the time. When I am standing before groups of activists of color, leading a dialogue with women, or sitting in intimate conversation with the young people who work with me, I want them to understand the urgency of self-confidence coupled with self-awareness. Our obligation is to trust our capacity to lead and to gather the tools and training necessary to do it well. We'll make mistakes, as everyone does, and ours will likely be judged more harshly. Yet our triumphs will also resound, and they will show the way for those who also doubt their calling.

What I learned from my family—my siblings who have achieved and the ones who struggle with drug addiction and incarceration—is that we are the architects of our futures. What my parents and family gave me are tools—tools that I use to fix problems and excavate opportunities and destroy obstacles. And, like any tool, if someone teaches you where to get it and how to use it, you can build something too. This book does not promise solutions, but I can show you the right tools and how to use them in the right way to make incremental progress that matters.

Beyond the question of how we push through is *what* we are pushing for. I am driven by a bitter hatred of poverty and the lack of mobility that keeps families in endless cycles of wasted ability. Kids should grow up as I did with a belief in their potential, no matter where they start or how differently they learn. I want to see the single Latino dad without a high school education decide he can start his own business. I want to register the Haitian immigrant to vote, because she deserves to have a say in her city's government. Knowing what drives your own passion is key, regardless of the scale or target. Writing poetry that finds a publisher or starting a day care center for homeless teen moms are both transformative ambitions. Finding out what you want to fight for is critical, and knowing how to get from thought to action is often easier said than done, so I also share exercises to help you figure it out for yourself. I encourage you to write out your own answers—on paper or in a digital format—and I promise, you'll surprise yourself in the process.

This book is for the outsider looking for the magic decoder ring for how to gain and hold power. But let's be clear—there isn't one. Instead, we have to understand and master the components of power: ambition, fear, money, failure, opportunity, and access. I break down how they function in leadership, and I offer stories to illuminate what works and what is harder to accomplish.

Leadership is hard. Convincing others—and often yourself—

that you have the answers to overcome long-standing obstacles takes a combination of confidence, insight, and sheer bravado. Finding ways to prevail, while bringing others along with you, is the core of being a good leader and the central tenet of *Lead from the Outside*. I wrote this book with the experiences and challenges in mind that might hinder *anyone* who exists outside the structure of traditional white male power—women, people of color, members of the LGBTQ+ community, those without money, and millennials ready to make a change.

By putting "otherness" at the center of the conversation, I do not intend to alienate anyone who has claims to privileges, but to draw a clearer map to the skills that have eluded the rest of us for so long. As minorities move closer to parity, we have to be ready to lead beyond what we might imagine. And that requires a handbook written for our experiences and challenges—a means to become the minority leaders who own our power and change our worlds.

One

DARE TO WANT MORE

I sit in the living room, a cozy space, warm in the early summer. I am perched on the edge of the sofa next to Valerie, the home's owner, a lovely black woman in her late forties. Across from us, seated close together on a wide settee meant for one, are her two children, a son and a daughter.

Politicians rarely visit their streets, which are nestled in a poorer community in south Georgia. Valerie beams with pride that both her children are headed to college in the fall. David, seventeen, plans to study criminology. Maya, eighteen, her belly round with her first child, intends to become a middle school teacher. Both newly graduated from high school, Maya will give birth in mere weeks and begin college months later, an unwed teen mother. Her intended school is more than three hours north of her home, so her mother will raise her newborn baby while she starts her freshman year.

Valerie speaks matter-of-factly about the coming challenge:

raising a new child just as hers leave the nest. Still, she is determined that both her children pursue degrees she never received. Maya, the mother-to-be, wonders aloud how she'll do so far away from home and her baby. Yet in the next breath, she explains how college will be best for her and her child. Their future success rests upon her.

I've come to their home as part of my campaign for governor, so I ask Valerie what she expects of someone like me. What can I do to help make lives like hers better? In her soft voice, she replies she just wants better options for financial aid for her children. They will succeed, she says, if they can afford to stay in school.

As I look around the modest home, passed down through generations, I understand both the pride and the desperation tangled in her response. She got them through and has given them the tools to carve out better lives for themselves. We chat more about the worries she's lived with all those years, our discussion turning to the crime and poverty in their community.

Then I ask Valerie what she wants. At first, all I get in response is a quizzical look that suggests I need to reconsider my bid for higher office. I repeat, "What do you want? For you? What secret dream do you have for yourself?" Her confused expression turns to one of surprise. "I don't know," she tells me. "I've been a cashier at the Piggly Wiggly for twenty years."

"You must want something," I probe, "something you'd like to do for you."

"A day care," she admits quietly. "I'd like to start a day care for unwed mothers, like my daughter. So more girls can finish school and pursue their dreams." But that ambition is beyond her—her body language, her tone of voice, her averted gaze speak louder than her words. I press her, but she demurs with a smile. "Let's just see what happens if you win the governor's job."

Valerie's house in south Georgia is not too different from the squat redbrick house where I grew up on South Street in Gulfport, Mississippi. An oak tree grew in our front yard, shadowing the front sidewalk, forbidding grass to grow beneath its shade. Pink azaleas bloomed each spring from bushes that flanked the front door. Our rented house, and the others set close by, teemed with children—all black, all working-class. We played in our postage-stamp yards, make-believing the fantastical. Superhero exploits. Cops and robbers. As we got older, we'd talk about moving to New Orleans or living in one of the mansions along the beachfront that lay less than five miles away, across the railroad tracks that ran in between our neighborhood and the wealthier environs. We dreamed of more, while our parents' lives centered around survival and making it from paycheck to paycheck. Instinctively, we understood that more had to be possible, even if we didn't know what to do to get there. These imaginings—these desires—are the root of ambition.

As adults, like Valerie, we tend to edit our desires until they fit our construction of who we're supposed to become. In such a world, I wouldn't dare dream of running for higher office, for mayor or governor or president. At least for now, Valerie sees herself retiring in twenty more years from the Piggly Wiggly as a cashier, rather than as a small business owner who helps a community raise its children. From our brief meeting, I could see she had the fire, albeit at a low burn, of a minority leader. She had ambition. She had a vision. But she didn't have the faith. And understandably so.

Whether we come from working-class neighborhoods or grow up comfortably middle-class, minorities rarely come of age explicitly thinking about what we want and how to get it.

People already in power almost never have to think about whether they belong in the room, much less if they would be listened to once inside. These men—and they are usually men and typically white—do not have to grapple with low expectations based on gender or race or class. Ambition for them begins with reminiscences of old times and older friendships or newer alliances. The ends have already been decided, with only the means to be discussed.

Most potential minority leaders feel the same lack of faith Valerie had, at least at some point in their evolution. We may not know how to get the first job, let alone make it to the big chair. We don't know how to take the leap from accepting our fates to actually changing them, and not just a little, but radically. Then there are those who simply do not know what they want. The drive to achieve burns inside, often without a clear target.

We want to "be something," but what that is remains hazy. Often, we cannot articulate our goals because they lie just beyond the reach of who we are supposed to be. Ambition's scale is irrelevant. What holds us back is not scope. It's fear.

And because we don't know what to call our dreams, don't know how to make them happen, or are pretty sure we'll be disappointed, we just stand still. But becoming a minority leader demands that we embrace ambition as our due.

In every sector where I've worked, I am driven by my ambition to encourage others to find their own dreams and exploit their potential. Whether I'm mentoring young people in organizations or speaking with those looking to forge new careers at midlife to explore their potential, the starting block is knowing what you want—and then wanting more. Run for office, take the helm at corporate boards, go back to college, or start a small business. Whatever the path, this book is designed to help locate our ambition and use it to create a path to leadership that does not bow to inner doubts or outside prejudices.

GETTING LOST IN POSSIBILITIES

During law school, one of my tax professors, Anne Alstott, hired me as a research assistant for a book she was coauthoring. As I combed through the reams of documents, I struggled to organize them into coherent and useful information. I tried to categorize by theme, by type, even by the size of the page, legal or standard. Lost in the sheer enormity of the project, I couldn't determine what was real and relevant versus what were merely interesting facts on a page.

When I presented my initial findings to Professor Alstott, she listened thoughtfully, asking the occasional question. At the end, she motioned me over to the whiteboard in her overstuffed office filled with books and monographs, and she told me the secret of how she approached research. Finding the truth requires three simple questions, she explained, and they must be answered in any investigation: (1) What is the problem? (2) Why is it a problem? (3) How do you solve it?

Finding, owning, and living one's ambition can feel a lot like that research project. In a world filled with options, we are paralyzed by choices. Or, worse, in so many cases, when we've been told our options are limited, we need to have the wherewithal to find our way to more. Rather than seeking outside expertise on whether we deserve what we want, we must look inward, not simply at our fears—of losing, of not being sufficient—but at the great difference living our ambitions can make if we succeed.

When we win, we achieve beyond ourselves. We become models for others, known and unknown, who see our victories as proof that they can win too. Even by simply embracing ambition, talking about it, trying and failing, we mentor others to see their potential. And by going beyond our own limits, we change the places we inhabit. We bring a fresh perspective to a company or a cause, a minority lens that expands and shifts how the work gets done. This is not news. Think of the companies scrambling to add women to their executive offices, people of color to their boards of directors. Or the nonprofit that adapts its mission because of the unique understanding it gains from incorporating the experience of those who have been outside.

When I work with young people and others seeking leadership positions, they are primed to jump to the third question, to the how of it, without understanding the what or the why. Some pick a place they want to land or a title they like and then expect teleportation. It may sound corny, but so many of us forget that finding and fulfilling ambition is truly a journey, and one that does not come with a map or GPS, especially for those of us on the outside looking to get in. The effort can be sweaty, teary, and messy as much as it can be rewarding and empowering. I call it the hard work of becoming more.

So what takes us beyond the dream to charting a new reality? What I've come to think of as Alstott's Queries, framed slightly differently, have become a cornerstone of how I frame almost every endeavor. Whether the dream is to run a company, run for office, or run a 5K—or even if your dream has not yet been discovered—the path to realizing ambition is the same:

1. What do I want?
2. Why do I want it?
3. How do I get there?

Before exploring these steps, it's crucial to understand and internalize our very right to even be ambitious. Because, for too many of us, we are stopped in our tracks before we begin because we don't believe we deserve to want more. And it is by wanting more that we begin.

I KNOW YOU ARE, BUT WHAT AM I

Early on, I had two experiences that helped me understand how to convert imaginings into ambition and realize that "too big" isn't a good reason not to try. The first occurred at the end of my junior year of high school. My public high school required all juniors to take the PSAT. Despite not having the tutors like some of my school friends, I'm a pretty good test taker and did well. My scores prompted an invitation to apply for a program I'd never heard of before—nor had any of my teachers. Still, I completed the extensive application for the Telluride Foundation because it promised a summer program away from home, and I thought it would be exciting to go to the north. I applied, and they selected me to attend TASP, which stands for Telluride Association Summer Program, a nerd summer camp for high achievers. I took the second plane ride of my life to Ithaca, New York, where I lived with fifteen of the smartest teenagers I'd ever met. For the first few days, I studiously avoided conversation, baffled by how I had been chosen to join them.

To a person, I could not compete. I wrote poetry for our high school journal. A girl there had published a collection. One was a concert-level violinist, and the others sounded like college professors. In our classroom sessions, I was called upon to answer questions, and I got more answers wrong than I ever had at Avondale High School. The other students referenced books I'd never read and scholars I hadn't heard of. Even casual conversation left me adrift, floundering to understand cultural references far beyond me. When I dared to introduce television into the mix, you'd have thought I cussed.

At the end of the first week, I called home, begging my parents to let me leave. I was out of my depth among these brainiacs, embarrassing myself every day. My parents, cruelly it seemed, refused. They demanded that I stay and learn as much as I could from the experience. My dad told me to get comfortable with not being anywhere near the smartest person in the room. I had to accept that I simply did not have the background or education the others did, and it was up to me to decide if that mattered.

The comment stung, but he was right. I had always been smart, but I needed to test myself against those who were smarter, more talented, and more accomplished. My ability to dream meant hearing about, and entering, worlds far different from my own. Athletes are encouraged to test themselves against better players. Proverbs tells us that iron sharpens iron. So too does ambition sharpen ambition. Dreams hone other dreams.

I stayed for the full summer, never once proving myself superior to anyone. Six weeks could not erase the difference in upbringing and access. But I learned from them, in our classes and beyond. I learned to mimic their sense of self-confidence and certainty. I didn't lie about what I knew, but I began to carry myself differently and speak with more authority.

Not everyone's ambitions will be world domination or Carnegie Hall, but we should be driven beyond what we know and feel safe doing. Ambition means pushing past simply what we are good at. The goal is to stretch ourselves, to explore our potential, even when we know we won't be first or the best. I sometimes advise people to watch what they fear, what makes them most nervous or feel the most self-protective—sometimes fear masks ambition. And unmasking it can unleash your drive.

Telluride introduced me to a world larger than my own, and then came Spelman College. A historically black college with a student body composed of 99 percent African American women, missionaries founded Spelman to help freed slave women embrace their liberty. Spelman operates as a four-year course on deprogramming black women stereotypes—the welfare queen, the hypersexualized Jezebel, being the lowest rung of the minority hierarchy—replaced by a parade of chief executive officers, public intellectuals, scientists, artists, and actors.

My mother tricked me into attending Spelman. A lifelong Southerner, I'd planned my escape by applying only to schools north of the Mason-Dixon Line. I had no interest in a women's college—a black one at that. Most of my classmates since kindergarten had been white students. Plus, as I hadn't been allowed to date until I was sixteen, the idea of a cloistered college experience held no appeal. But Mom guilted me into applying, reminding me that she hadn't had the opportunity to attend due to her family's poverty. When I was admitted, she convinced me to take advantage of a day off from school to visit. I found myself astonished by the incredible diversity of a black women's college, a stone's throw away from a black men's college, Morehouse College. In the end, my visit persuaded me to add Spelman to the list of colleges I might attend. I put the names into a cup: Spelman, Swarthmore, Sarah Lawrence, and Vassar. Spelman came out three times, and I sent in my acceptance.

At Spelman, I had the second experience that moved me closer to knowing what I wanted for my future. Suddenly, I found myself seeing how much blacks could achieve, beyond the handful of television shows I'd watched. My new classmates were the daughters of politicians and famous lawyers and corporate leaders. One of my closest friends mentioned in passing that she had the U.S. surgeon general's home number. While several of us came from more modest means, our college expected us to dream beyond our narrow understanding of what we could be. I threw myself into college life, hungry to become this new superwoman: the Breaker of Stereotypes, Destroyer of Black Woman Myths. I was now in a context that included people of color, women no less, who had confidence that they could succeed.

I learned at Telluride and Spelman that I was allowed to craft my future. Those experiences had quelled some of my self-doubt; but even then, I pretended to be more fearless than I felt. I tried out for the spring play, despite my personal worries that I wasn't as sylphlike as my castmates. I ran for vice president of the Student Government Association as a sophomore, clearly lacking the years of experience my predecessors and my opponent had. I persevered and won, despite my shortcomings and despite my own inner doubts, which I managed to keep at bay, though just barely.

This is where Alstott's Queries, the what, why, and how, become most critical. Once we accept that we deserve to want more and we understand how giving birth to ambition requires knowing ourselves better, we're ready to actually start figuring out what lights us up and then plotting out our pathways to get it.

WHAT'S LOVE GOT TO DO WITH IT

When I was eighteen, I spent an evening in our college computer lab, the fluorescent lights crackling overhead reflecting off the near-green screen. While the few other students there on a week-night likely toiled over papers, I'd been driven from my dorm room by what felt like an urgent project. In the lab that night, I created a spreadsheet. The Lotus 1-2-3 document laid out my life plans for the next forty years. Seriously.

As a teenager, I'd read about John D. Rockefeller, who'd kept careful lists of each goal and painstakingly mapped every moment of his life. Since he'd gone on to become one of the wealthiest men in the world, the idea of writing down my lofty goals struck me as the right approach. The act also allowed me to plan rather than act, to set future goals and avoid hard choices in the here and now. Whether scribbled into diaries or typed onto a computer, the act of writing down what I wanted became an ego's Christmas list. Lots of stuff that you know Santa will never deliver.

I hadn't come to the computer lab because of a sudden burst of inspiration. Quite the contrary—my heart had been broken. Chad, the second boy I'd ever dated, decided to end our relationship. As he pointed out in painstaking detail, I had not been a good girlfriend. He told me I had no passion, no capacity for love beyond my pursuits. Between student government and the spring play and classes, I'd not invested as much time in the actual work of our relationship. To be honest, I spared our relationship less attention because I didn't know how to do it well. Extracurricular experiences seemed much easier than navigating the emotions of romance. As aggressive as I could be in secular pursuits, affairs of the heart perplexed me, and I focused on what I understood.

Still, when he broke up with me, my confidence shattered.

All around me, young men and women managed to effectively date one another. My abject failure—and I believed at the time it was all mine—surely signaled only one truth: I should focus on my professional life.

Fueled by sorrow and outrage, I decided to map out my life that night. A cold, comforting spreadsheet seemed to be the best way to focus on what I was good at, particularly by Chad's estimation. The sheet contained four columns: year, age, job, and tasks. And they represented very different facets of myself. I was determined to embrace them all.

I intended at age twenty-four to write a best-selling spy novel like the stories I'd been captivated by in the Bond movies and on *General Hospital*. I'd organized my college class schedule around the exploits of Anna Devane and Robert Scorpio, denizens of the fictional town of Port Charles and spies for the WSB, the World Security Bureau. Despite watching these shows since childhood, and every Bond movie, none of the characters on my beloved soap looked like me, and precious few blockbuster thriller novels had black women on their covers. My mother, a librarian for most of my childhood, had taught us how books shaped our sense of the possible. For me, for other young black girls, I wanted to write books that showed them to be as adventurous and attractive as any white woman.

By thirty, I would be a millionaire running a corporation whose purpose I had not yet figured out. Having grown up as working poor, I decided having money was next. With my new wealth, I would help my parents buy their first house, a Kennedyesque compound on the shores of the Mississippi Gulf Coast. Like the perennial winners in the Publishers Clearing House commercials, I dreamed big.

Fame and fortune had been put on the docket, and only power needed a slot. Lucky for me, I had also decided I wanted to be the mayor of Atlanta by the age of thirty-five. Of the dreams I had for myself, becoming mayor struck me as the most ambitious. I'd read a handful of prominent black suspense writers, and Oprah had already begun her path to great wealth, so the road to items 1 and 2 seemed doable, albeit incredibly challenging. Although Atlanta had a black mayor, no black woman had led a major city in the nation, so I allocated fifteen years of prep time. All this while sitting in Spelman's computer lab late into the night.

Though my list was exhaustive, and driven by grief and the need to reclaim my sense of self, the results were vitally important. I began to access what I wanted. I might not get there in all those arenas (though I have come close!), and my specific ambitions might not endure, but that wasn't the point. The point was that I was letting myself experience the feeling of wanting itself: acknowledging in print—in a formal spreadsheet even—that I could see myself thriving in the world, that I was allowed to dare to want.

This audacity of ambition starkly contrasted with the place where I'd grown up. As a high school senior, I had a solid GPA and a list of notable achievements, but I wasn't terribly outgoing and never had been. In childhood games with my sisters, I'd pretended to be a tycoon, a superhero, or President of the World, but those dreams held as much reality as an episode of *Dynasty*. In my real life, my natural introversion meant that I had few close friends and I rarely socialized outside of school.

Reading served as the spark for my imagination of a different future. I rarely met a professional person in daily life, though there was the occasional doctor or professor at the college where my mother served as librarian. And I certainly didn't see them in my neighborhood where most people worked hourly-wage jobs. Because I didn't know people who had grand dreams, moving beyond make-believe seemed harder and harder as I grew older and games lost their allure.

After hours in front of the computer that night, I reread my spreadsheet and surprised myself by laughing out loud. Suddenly I saw the obnoxiousness of the list of to-dos that I'd painstakingly plotted. Part of me laughed at the sheer length of the list and the incredible heights I wanted to reach in so many arenas. But I also laughed with self-mockery. Despite being surrounded by Spelman's daughters of accomplishment, I had no clear way to do any of what I'd imagined.

My finger lingered over the Delete key, but in the end, I pressed Save. While my boyfriend's derision compelled me out of my room, the project was mine alone. In the lab that night, I realized a core tenet behind deciding what you want: don't stop yourself with the logic of possibility.

Logic is a seductive excuse for setting low expectations. Its cool, rational precision urges you to believe that it makes sense to limit yourself. And when your goal means you'll be the first, or one of the few, as I desired, logic tells you that if it were possible, someone else would have done it by now.

Whether the hesitation comes from well-meaning counselors or skeptical bosses or from that little voice in your head, embracing ambition means learning not to listen too closely to anyone. Ambition should be heady stuff. It should make your neck itch and your palms sweat. Or, if you're lucky, ambition may bring a smile to your face. The smile of actually seeing a different, bigger future.

I DON'T WANT WHAT I HAVEN'T GOT (AND OTHER LIES)

Over the next several years, I curated my spreadsheet like Gollum tending his Precious, but I also continued to question the rightness of my reach. While I would proudly tell certain friends of my dreams, the sheer boldness of my ambitions gnawed at me. And even carefully organized spreadsheets can't predict the future, I would find out. But they—or another form of planning—are more than an avoidance technique. Knowing what lights you up and embracing what you daydream about are the first steps.

What comes next to turn ambition into action is understanding the why. When you understand the roots of your dreams, you will have deeper insight into why you want what you want. You'll be able to either strengthen your resolve or clarify if the target you've chosen is the right one. What you want to do and why you want to do it should align.

I can easily trace my goal of becoming mayor to my freshman year of college. Through my volunteer work, I'd already regularly attended city council meetings and understood the importance of a mayor's decisions in tackling the poverty in Atlanta. When I first added the goal to my spreadsheet, I held a superficial dream of being in charge of the city. But later in that spring of 1992, America exploded when the Rodney King verdict was announced in late April. In Los Angeles, the city teemed with a violence that had not been seen in decades. In downtown Atlanta, where I attended school, young black men and women smashed windows, overturned cars, and ransacked the city. For my part, I joined with fellow students in a silent march down to city hall from the Atlanta University Center, known to Atlantans as the AUC.

The AUC—the nation's largest contiguous consortium of historically black colleges and universities—included Clark Atlanta University, Morehouse College, Morris Brown College, and Spelman College, as well as the Interdenominational Theological Center and the Morehouse School of Medicine. The AUC possesses a proud tradition of civic engagement, as the college home of luminaries such as Martin Luther King Jr., Marian Wright Edelman, and Walter Francis White. I wanted to do their legacy justice, and I felt called to continue their work.

Yet, although I helped lead the peaceful protest, the gesture felt emptier than I expected. I understood what drove those angry young people to hurl bottles and shout epithets. Some of the protesters lived in the oldest housing projects in Georgia, stolid rust-brown buildings situated across the street. For those who lived a stone's throw beyond the privileged gates of Spelman and Morehouse, of Clark Atlanta and Morris Brown, their violence expressed an impotence and outrage too explosive for dignified marches.

I revered the civil rights movement and appreciated the laws that granted us the right to ride buses, to sit at lunch counters, to cast ballots. But the slowness of real change fueled the riots' intensity, from coast to coast. Decades later, inequality still ravaged poor and black communities. Then toss in the continued international struggle to end apartheid, the skyrocketing incarceration rates that scooped up too many of black folks' cousins, and a youth poverty rate that defied the wealth of the era. I knew the truth behind their rage.

In the wake of the Rodney King verdict, college kid and disenfranchised neighbor alike, we reviled the decision of twelve jurors to ignore the videotaped evidence of racist cops. Yet the riots posed only a distant distraction for a number of my fellow college students. On our campuses, final exams were beginning and students unmoved by or inattentive to the social unrest hurried around the AUC to take their last tests. They had little interest in the Korean grocery stores being looted as frustrations boiled between neighbors or in the black businesses destroyed in a blaze of Molotov cocktails. Amid the destruction, most of the talented tenths of the AUC ignored calls for marches in favor of turning in term papers. As college students, we'd been trained to believe that our education separated us from those outside our classrooms, and we would do our best work for everyone by acing our tests, not by direct action.

Still, as the police moved into our area of the city to quell the unrest, a strange thing happened. Tear gas canisters rained down onto our college quads, vile smoke flooding the open spaces. Across the street, similar bombs exploded in the eyes of Section 8 housing dwellers. The police swarmed onto our campuses and the housing projects both, and suddenly, any distinctions between our two worlds were meaningless. The police only saw congregations of young blacks, and race became a unifying marker of guilt.

The Atlanta police cordoned off the interstate exit leading to the area, and marked cars stationed around the area prevented anyone from leaving. Trapped on campus, I fumbled for a way to act, unaware that the next few hours would change the course of my life. Watching the news, I heard false reports about why the area was under siege and facile explanations for complex social problems. After seething and talking back to the television set,

I called the most offensive station to demand they do a better job of telling the story. The person who answered my call refused to take my message to her superiors. She politely hung up on me, and I less politely called back. Just before her third hang-up, she snapped that I was tying up the line.

Truth telling, especially stories about minorities, matters. We are so frequently viewed through lenses that encourage the majority to fear us or to distrust us. That afternoon, I watched as an entire city—a nation in microcosm—heard from their news reporters to once again be afraid of black people. To believe us all to be destructive, angry vandals rather than complex human beings who had seen in a single verdict an indictment of our humanity. If Rodney King could be beaten on tape, and his known police assailants exonerated, what would stop others from furthering our treatment as subhuman?

Quickly, I looked up the numbers to all the television stations. Before the advent of 24/7 cable news, most people got their sense of what was happening from just four networks. Worried that their stories would cement a narrative about blacks in Atlanta, I scribbled down the numbers on several sheets of paper. I went up and down the halls of my dorm and organized fellow students to begin calling the television stations to extend our protests. Like the march, the act of making calls didn't require extraordinary courage, but dialing phones gave my friends and me a way to help. As I'd learned from my parents, protest takes on multiple forms. And, as I'd also learned, being black did not change with zip code or by entering the elite gates of a private college. But a phone call to a newsroom could change the conversation, if only for thirty seconds. Soon, the television stations demanded a name to go along with the phone calls jamming their lines. I flippantly told my friends to just give the news stations my name.

Again, this was not a premeditated or complicated strategic act, which we often associate with ambition. The why of ambition can be born in a moment. The decision to act, to reach, can be in response to an external crisis. Or, a fleeting idea can ignite you and point you toward something bigger than you are. The key is to be aware of what is going on both around you and inside you, staying open to opportunities to authentically express what you believe and who you are.

As our phone strategy stretched on, I watched the footage of our campuses surrounded by cop cars. Rage dueled with sadness as I saw the treatment of black students and residents in a city ostensibly run by and for black folks. In the end, we were all the same to those in charge.

My reaction to the equity of suspicion shamed me. If I was honest with myself, I was upset because all my borrowed trappings of elitism meant nothing as Atlanta burned. That disquiet stayed with me the rest of the day, scratching at my conscience. I had to confront the why of my outrage and how I would deal with its aftermath. I needed to probe my own sense of privilege. But, for the moment, I needed to focus on correcting the record.

Unfortunately, our phone jams of the TV stations had no effect on their coverage. However, by the early evening, a television producer invited me to join a community town hall to be simulcast across the city. I assume they picked me because of my prolific phone calls (and I was the only real name they had).

I arrived at the studio where I met Mayor Maynard Jackson for the first time. I had seen him before from afar, but I had not met the legendary man who, at the age of thirty-five, had become the first African American mayor of Atlanta and of any major city in the South. Race had driven him—both the reality that blacks could control a major city and the history of how the city had treated blacks. Nearly twenty years later, a different issue of race stirred me now. Black people occupied the mayor's office and much of the city council and held high positions in commerce and civic life. Despite the visible progress Mayor Jackson's legacy had yielded, race continued to define many of our problems. Poverty, struggling schools, and decaying communities plagued black faces in a city that had black leadership.

Awed to be in the presence of such a powerful leader, a black one no less, I listened as he offered his analysis of the riots. While he acknowledged the profound disappointment of the verdict, he decried the reaction. Then he offered choice words for the young demonstrators who had wreaked havoc on his city. As he spoke, my awe turned to anger. This powerful man who stood at the head of a city known for its civil disobedience seemed to hold no sympathy for those who found no other outlet for their despair. So he had sent the police to public housing and to our campuses.

Anger, like any strong emotion, can move us beyond our normal comfort zones. In front of cameras and the crowd, I demanded to know what the mayor had done for the dispossessed youth of Atlanta. For the undereducated who turned to gangs and drugs. For the impoverished who worried more about their next meal than their grades.

With a boldness that surprised me, I excoriated his record and scoffed at his leadership. If I'd thought more deeply before I stood, I might have held my tongue. But I had shed much of my fear of not being right during that Telluride summer program. And since I was there, in the halls of power, being relentless seemed in order. In this moment I had access to power, a voice, and a question. Sometimes the why of ambition can only be discovered in a nervy action that cuts against our natural instincts. Maybe it is asking the question in a meeting that no one else has—and that you think may expose your ignorance. Or pushing back on a superior. Presenting an idea others have mocked. Speaking up does not create ambition, but the act can help you to clear away what might be blocking your view.

In return, Mayor Jackson lectured me on how far the city had come, about the sacrifices made by earlier generations. Then he looked down at me from his very imposing height and promised to give my concerns due consideration.

And the mayor kept his promise. A few months later, I began work as the research assistant at the Mayor's Office of Youth Services for the City of Atlanta during my sophomore year in college. Like a lot of college students, I worked while going to school. In my case, the job changed my life, channeling my worries about injustice into a place designed to guarantee access. I had not been naïve about government's power, but on the inside, I saw firsthand how government, though an imperfect tool, provided a way for an introvert like me to raise my voice and act.

Those two days in late April imprinted themselves on me, sharpening a childhood that had prepared me to wonder about how I would help my people. I didn't come from a political family, had never had a full conversation with a politician, even when I had attended zoning hearings at city hall. And though I had typed in my goal of becoming mayor weeks before, those days revealed why the role could be so vital. What I had were opportunities that those outside Spelman's gates did not, and I had a responsibility to do more because I'd made it inside.

For the next decade, I followed the plans on my spreadsheet. I failed miserably at becoming a millionaire by thirty, but I met enough of my metrics to be in a pretty good position. According to my calculations and the plaudits of those who knew my goals, I was on track to achieve my life's ambition: becoming mayor of Atlanta.

Turns out, I was wrong.

I don't want to be the mayor—of anywhere. I focused on a job title and work that seemed to meet my dreams, but the job itself should never have been the dream. Ambition should be more than a title or a position. I'd focused on the what, not the why, and for more than a decade, I organized my life around that what. I understand now that knowing the real reason for your ambition allows you to figure out if a different path will get you there.

This is a distinction of immense difference. At its most complex, ambition should be an animation of soul. Not simply a job, but a disquiet that requires you to take action. For me, my ambition owed as much to my desire to serve communities isolated by poverty and racism as it did to my refusal to believe either had to be permanent fixtures in our lives. I latched on to the role of mayor as the clearest path to what I imagined could be accomplished. But realizing the why of my ambition allowed me to alter course and explore new roles that could accomplish the outcomes even more effectively.

We all set our sights on jobs we want, titles we covet. But, like dating the wrong person, we have to learn to understand what is truly for us and be willing to break up to find the real thing. We stay too long in jobs, hoping the work changes, rather than hunting for the right fit. Ambition means being proactive. The executive who becomes a writer. The teacher who becomes a banker. The shipyard worker who becomes a minister. Those are our inspirations. Being willing and able to change course means honing our ambition to the point where we know when it's time to move on or up.

Becoming mayor isn't the only ambition I had wrong. Rather than writing the seminal espionage novel, I became a romantic suspense writer. Turns out, once I put pen to paper, I finally understood I wanted to write stories about women who looked like me, ones whose lives were as exciting as anything I'd read or seen on a movie screen. I didn't have to be Ian Fleming to tell those tales. When I let go of my fixation on crafting the pièce de résistance of spy craft fiction, I found a story—and a career—that I had never imagined.

I first ran for office because I understood that government has a tremendous capacity to help people unlock their own potential, and I wanted a job where I could foster change for families like mine. Families who want more than entry-level jobs that pay the lowest wages. I want to lead a state that does more than survive—doing okay by some, and not so great by too many of us. That means becoming governor, although no black woman has ever held the job in American history.

I have absolute clarity on the role I want next, but as you consider what wakes you up, don't discount the importance of having no real answer to the question. Indecision, effectively applied, is a great way to figure it out. Give yourself the space to explore *why* you don't know what you want. Is it that you are afraid of the scope of your dreams? Or that you have too many dreams to pick just one? Maybe you haven't seen enough of the world to know what you want. Perhaps the hesitation lies somewhere in between. Finding your ambition demands that you allow yourself the time and energy to understand what holds you back from defining what you really want.

I am a living example of the fact that there is no glory in having only one supreme goal. Too few books on achieving your dreams acknowledge that we are multifaceted beings with many different talents and interests. Society sometimes chides us to be focused on one goal, one passion, one ambition. It starts in college when we're told to pick a major. Or think about the suspicion we feel when an actor announces a Christmas album or a politician writes a romance novel. "Jack of all trades, master of none" is the unkindest cut.

Benjamin Banneker, astronomer, clockmaker, and abolitionist, who laid out the plans for Washington, DC, also carried on a heated correspondence with Thomas Jefferson over the abolition of slavery. Professor of mathematics Dalip Singh Saund broke barriers as an Indian American who fought to secure the right for Indian immigrants to become US citizens in 1949. Forced to be a farmer for much of his time in the United States, he later became a US congressman, the first Indian to serve. Think of Beyoncé and Lin-Manuel Miranda, who master multiple arts, securing Grammys, Oscar nominations, and Tonys for their works. But also, consider the dedicated nurse who spends every weekend at the animal shelter, driven by an ambition to treat the suffering.

It's been twenty years and my spreadsheet, now upgraded to Excel, has been edited several times. Swap in or out a dozen jobs, many I never imagined at eighteen, and I better understand why the spreadsheet is so important to me.

While I climbed my way toward what I thought was the mayor's office, I also honed my skills as an attorney. I learned the law under the tutelage of exceptional lawyers, including Teresa Wynn Roseborough, a brilliant woman who had become the first black woman partner at our law firm.

One afternoon I sat in her spacious office, the sunlight from the twenty-first-floor windows streaming in and lighting the room with a pearlescent glow. My digs on the twenty-third floor of the law firm were not too shabby, especially for a third-year associate. I had a window, a secretary, and a path to partnership. My job at Sutherland Asbill & Brennan came as close to marrying my interests as any legal role could. As a tax attorney, I had burrowed my way into a tiny subgroup that specialized in tax-exempt organization law. Shorthand: I helped nonprofits and charities but got paid like a corporate attorney. Our clients ranged from multinational NGOs to well-financed corporations that did business with nonprofits to universities and hospitals.

Yet I had grown restless and thought more and more about my spreadsheet and the political goals I recorded there. I sat in Teresa's office and shared my plan for how I would move from my perch on the twenty-third floor to city hall. Instead of the approving nod to my careful planning, she challenged my focus on the mayor's job. Was it a broad enough platform for the visions I held? Did I only want to affect Atlanta, or should my ambition aim even higher?

When you decide what you want and why you want it, take action immediately. Do not wait for an invitation to act. I promise you, the letter is not in the mail. Know what you want. Know why you want it. Know how you will achieve it. Then get started. Take a class, apply for a job, read a book about it. But do something that moves you forward at a constant pace. If you can walk away for days, weeks, or years at a time, it is not an ambition—it's a wish. Wishes feel good and rarely come true. Ambition, on the other hand, fuels your days and refuses to be ignored. It challenges your sense of self and fulfills your sense of wonder. So pay attention.

And get to work.

AMBITION EXERCISE

We tend to measure our passions by their likelihood of success, not the joy and excitement they bring. Use this exercise to reveal if you are being honest about what your ambitions truly are.

You can find this and all the exercises in this book online at minorityleaderbook.com/exercises.pdf. I encourage you to download the sheets and fill them out. It will make a world of difference.

What would you do if you had unlimited money?

If you could do any five things for the rest of your life, what would they be?

1.

2.

3.

4.

5.

What else would you ask for?

Rank your top five activities from most appealing to least appealing.

Rank activities	Most appealing qualities	Least appealing qualities
1.		
2.		
3.		
4.		
5.		

Would you swap out anything from the "what else" list for what you wrote as your top five activities? Why or why not?

Two

FEAR AND OTHERNESS

There's a speech I give about leadership, where I talk about the big F: Fearlessness. For several minutes, I exhort my audience to be daring, to try the improbable, to ignore the doubts of nay-sayers and their own worries. But, I am also aware that what I blithely diagnose in my talk ignores a more fundamental barrier for those attempting to assert power and leadership in spaces of privilege. The talk serves a practical purpose, to encourage my audience to take bold action despite the panic in their throats and the sweat on their brows, because, I advise, the goal on the other side of anxiety is worth the pain. Problem is, my advice is a superficial solution—a pithy remedy for a fundamental problem whose roots dig deep into the soul and confidence. I make light of this dark emotion, as those are the limits of fifteen-minute speeches. But I understand we cannot gain real power until we acknowledge fear's potency.

Fear is a paralyzing force that twists deep in the gut, churning out anxiety and reasons not to act. Its seductive logic convinces us that now is not our time and winning is not our right. Worse, fear takes on a numbing familiarity, becoming as automatic as brushing our teeth or checking text messages. The transition from moments of anxiety into habit begins young, when we are cautioned against action because of harsh, unforeseen consequences. I don't mean the healthy warnings about not talking to strangers or keeping tiny fingers away from dangerous objects. No, I refer to the hesitation to speak up in class because the teacher only calls on boys. The reluctance to sit at the lunch table lest the mean girls point and laugh. Or, worse, getting beaten up by neighborhood kids because of the way we talk or act or who we befriend.

But, sometimes, the call is coming from inside our heads. We worry about embarrassment, about failure, about capacity. That our raised hand in class will actually be called upon, and the wrong answer will emerge loud and stupid. If we apply for that college, that job, that promotion, rejection will most certainly follow.

Later, as we grow older, we internalize the voice of this fear spoken in pronouncements of our inadequacy when it comes to leadership: we're not going to win, and now isn't our turn. Fear is validated when we do apply for advancement, but in response we don't get the thick envelope inviting us to join. Instead, the one letter we receive denies access because we lack the pedigree or experiences to make it beyond the barricade. We're not fit to hold authority because no one like us has held it before, and the powers that be do not intend to take a chance on us.

Worse, our sense that we're not quite like the others has no clearer messenger than the well-meaning friend who praises our intellect, then mentions in a sad sigh how *smart* isn't enough.

You've probably had the conversation, the one where you explain why the system is rigged against you. And, rather than agree this is a problem, your companion tries to justify why you won't break through. Conditioning doesn't just happen to us—it happens around us, touching everyone and everything. We learn not to want, not to expect, because we're trained not to see ourselves as more than what we've been told to be. Thus, fear becomes as familiar as air, an automatic caution against bucking the system.

The words aren't often spoken in polite company, but the reality becomes reinforced every time we see power in action, and it looks nothing like us. Fear is instinctive, but it is also a learned response. When we see leadership denied because the person reaching for more doesn't look the part or is too different from who has come before, the apprehension makes complete sense. When I was in high school, my parents were called into the United Methodist ministry. For my mom, the call was more difficult due to the antipathy she faced from male pastors. I remember one evening at a revival service, the church's pastor welcomed all the visiting preachers to join him at the pulpit. We looked to my parents, who remained seated with us in the pews. Earlier, the pastor had warned her she'd be excluded. No women ministers allowed. Always, my father too refused the invitation. To this day, I recall the stoic look on my mother's face as she watched her peers accorded a respect she was due but did not receive. For her, this exclusion occurred regularly, her leadership denied because of sexism, practiced in a holy space.

Even now, as I run for governor, dear friends I have known for decades have pulled back, murmuring platitudes about how right they think I am for the office, but adding, "Georgia's not ready for a black woman." In the first few weeks of my campaign, this mantra became routine as I called literally hundreds of friends, acquaintances, and admirers. With each warning against the arrogance of my candidacy, my certitude about running for this office became shakier. What if they saw something, knew something I didn't? Concern morphed into a constant disquiet that had me second-guessing a plan I'd been painstakingly building for more than a decade.

I became more and more afraid, reluctant to do the work of campaigning because I didn't want to pick up the phone and hear another person I admired tell me my skin color and gender would be my undoing. I'm good on the phone, but suddenly I was afraid to dial. I prayed as the call rang through that no one would answer. And sitting on a park bench after hearing from a mentor that he wouldn't support me, I nearly quit.

Fear is real, insidious, and damaging. But it can be defeated if we are willing to name it, own it, and use it.

NAME IT AND KNOW IT

For minority leaders to move forward, we must oftentimes first confront layers of anxiety holding us back. To achieve power, to become effective leaders, we must name what scares us and acknowledge what scares those who are afraid of us. The threat isn't always external, and the solutions can be both painful and permanent. Fear must be deconstructed and understood because otherwise we miss opportunities. We cede authority to those who do not understand or care about our needs. We verify stereotypes and deepen the shallow understanding of our capabilities. Without a hard, tough understanding of fear, the reality is, nothing changes.

A deep apprehension for many of us is the stereotype threat: the idea that we will always be judged by the worst example of someone in our community. The way people of color flinch when someone who looks like them shows up on the eleven o'clock news and the silent cry of thanks when the mug shot isn't one of us.

The corollary to the stereotype threat is what I call the authenticity conundrum. Sometimes, our anxiety stems from worry about how our minority status lumps us in with everyone else, erasing our individuality and raising the question: how do we retain a sense of identity without abandoning the true similarities shared with our kindred groups?

Beyond the fears of who we are and how we are seen, minorities must grapple with the fear that if we're *too* good, we alienate ourselves from our communities and safety nets. Put another way, wanting more than we're supposed to forces us to confront not only the possibility of failure but also the responsibility of success. If I want too much, will I be able to do it? And the quieter question, what if too many people notice that I'm good at this? Being afraid of success is a real fear too.

Recently, I got a call from an acquaintance who planned to relocate back to Atlanta from New York. We chatted about mutual friends, the bitter defeat of any number of Atlanta sports teams, the unrelenting heat of a Georgia summer. After a while, we meandered toward the reason for her call.

Marielena, a smart, savvy, thirty-three-year-old Latina woman, had a problem. After a decade in finance, she'd hit upon a brilliant solution to a consistent problem in her industry. She wanted to strike out on her own, but no one she knew had ever launched a company. A barbershop or neighborhood café, perhaps, but nothing destined for the Fortune 500. All the books she'd read urged boldness. Still, in the fine print, nearly every success story began with doting parents willing to lend a garage and $10,000 or a network of well-heeled friends able to chip in to a start-up fund. And most were filled with examples of male entrepreneurs, the great majority white.

Because she came from a working-class family, her relatives could not help her. Marielena shied away from asking her few friends with means, afraid they'd scoff at her lofty goal. Instead, quite logically, she'd taken her proposal to a bank, only to be denied because she lacked adequate outside financing. The banker had asked her for examples of competitors in her field and who led them, and Marielena found herself naming man after man, many from the books she'd studied. Marielena watched as his smile got tighter and tighter. Finally, his point made, in a pseudo-friendly voice, the banker recommended that she share her idea with upper management and keep her day job.

I asked how I could help, revved up to strategize about how to respond to the banker or find alternative capital. I had started a few successful ventures, so I had ideas about end-running the chauvinism. But that wasn't why she'd called. She'd decided to abandon her vision and instead take a lateral role in her current company in Atlanta. Marielena wanted introductions. I offered her a list of colleagues to whom I would happily introduce her. But I couldn't let go of her story.

I asked Marielena why she chose not to try other roads for support of her start-up. After dancing around the answer, she finally said, "How could I solve a problem that no one else had? Who would believe me?"

I nudged again, "And?"

"The idea is too big," she confessed.

Too big. She could have said too foreign, outside her experience, not for the likes of her. She named the reason she stopped herself, but at its core, the barrier to her taking the next step was fear. But knowing what we want means, often, wanting more than we're supposed to.

Fear is a common obstacle. Men experience fear—even white, powerful men who have rarely known the word "no." But for the marginalized groups—those whose skin tone, gender, geography, or bank account signals "lesser than"—it can become a permanent companion eating away at confidence, ambition, relationships, and dreams.

Everyone is afraid of something. Yet the complexity of minority fear cannot be dismissed by saying "don't be afraid" or "let it go." Our trepidation is often grounded in stories we've heard about some brave soul losing a job, a house, a loan, or, if we look to the history of movements led by the courageous, their lives. Not every act of courage has life-or-death consequences, but leadership necessarily moves the actor closer to higher stakes.

Minority fears have distinct branches that get tangled up: stereotypes intermingle with authenticity and achievement. Will I get a shot because of who I am? If I fail, do I bring down everyone who looks like me? If I'm too successful, will my people celebrate me or shun me? How do I integrate into the world where I am an outsider, yet not move too far away from the places that make me who I am?

Navigating power is difficult enough without adding the dimensions of otherness to the mix, but that's our reality. Traditionally, only white men operate wholly as individuals, each person's actions attributable to him alone. For everyone else—and I do mean everyone else—we operate as part of a reductive collective. Women. Blacks. Latinos. Asians. Native Americans. Gays. Working class. Poor. Our successes may have individual origin stories (unless attributed to affirmative action), but our missteps become one more thread in the story of why we're not in charge.

MAKE FEAR YOUR NEW FRIEND

There's a famous experiment about kittens placed in a box with bars that gave off a mild shock. These kittens tried to escape at first, always blocked by the impenetrable bars. Then they stopped trying. One day, the scientists removed the bars and the kittens were free to escape, to explore the wider world beyond their box. But the animals stayed put. Even with the bars gone, they'd become too used to the limitations and were fearful of the shocks. So they stayed stuck inside, bound by nothing more than fear and memory.

Fighting fear demands sacrifice, and anyone who says otherwise is a liar. Worse, the sacrifice may not be yours to bear. Others often pay a price for those minorities who seek to break beyond the limitations we are told to accept. So understanding the contours and consequences of fear is critical and making the decision to go for it demands understanding who might become collateral damage. Maintaining friends, staying close to family, having intimacy with significant others, even finding a significant other can become infinitely more complex when power is in play. But, often, it's the fear, not the power, creating the great-est harm.

Confronting fear, breaking past the instinct to avoid pain or threat, cannot be avoided, not if what we want is leadership. Tak-ing charge, making decisions—these are not considered the prov-ince of our kind. Stories of overcoming fear, of risk-taking, of something ventured and gained have a common star: white men who defy odds or are presumably smarter, faster, better than the rest of us. On their broad shoulders alone can life-altering success be carried.

Television shows, still today, are chock-full of white men, with minority supporting characters, all toiling toward the realization of a great ambition as a surgeon, lawyer, president, or cop. Whether the hero in question wears a cape or sits at the head of a company, minorities constantly receive the message that ambition is not for *us*.

And the message is reinforced from other corners: the well-meaning family who wants to protect us; the colleague who thought she was different and got burned. Reasons abound for why we are tripped up by low expectations, why we fear our fail-ure is imminent and victory unlikely. What's worse is that we learn to measure our own passions by the extent of our fear, not the joy and excitement they may bring. Over time, we've been cautioned not to overreach in a meeting, not to volunteer for a task, not to take ourselves seriously. In this way, fear becomes comfortable and familiar and no longer as dangerous or elusive as success.

People are always in search of the familiar that validates their own privilege and position. We adapt how we behave to the expectations of what folks see and therefore expect. At a black women's college, I pretended to be more social, more stylish than

I was—driven as much by internalized racism as any societal pressures from my new community. At Yale and at the law firm where I subsequently worked, I pretended mannerisms that I copied from those who'd grown up with privilege, hoping that imitation would become reality. But buying pricey purses and scoffing at foods I'd never eaten failed to change the fact that I was different, and pretending otherwise was a waste of time. My responsibility, our responsibility as minority leaders, is to demonstrate to those in power the value in our difference. Minority leaders work to challenge conventional expectations without burying personal identity and cultural distinctiveness.

The problem is we might lose out. Owning fear of our otherness does not make it magically vanish. Admitting fear of not being sufficient will not erase false impressions of our capacity. All the "-isms" will remain, and those who hold prejudices will do a fantastic job all on their own of undermining our paths to success.

But unexamined fear has real consequences too. Marielena later shared with me that her boss had taken her idea to higherups, who planned to implement it and create a new division— which a male colleague at her level would be promoted to lead. To her credit, she protested the decision, but her boss explained that her idea wasn't proprietary because she'd told others about it, including him. When the company's leadership decided to act, they decided her male counterpart showed more initiative. More courage. Apparently, during her tenure at the company, Marielena had undercut herself by downplaying her smarts, questioning her qualifications, and conceding rather than fighting. She was a victim of discrimination, yes, but also of her own fears.

Marielena, like many of us, cut herself off before anyone else could. There's nothing like a vision of failure to quell ambition.

Marielena, battered by both external and personal doubts, invited fear to take the lead. Instead of repeating her mistakes, we must identify our own uncertainties and doubts and develop the habit of rebutting them. Like muscle memory, turning fear into a companion rather than the driver of our worst decisions helps improve how we lead.

USING FEAR FOR FUEL

Fear and otherness are real, and fear *of* otherness is pervasive. But fear can be defeated if we learn how to use it. In order to succeed as a leader, no matter the arena, we must fully recognize and acknowledge that race, gender, and pedigree are markers that strongly shape our impressions of ourselves and others. Stereotypes are shorthand for information. But they are also vessels for the anxiety we have of the unknown or the different.

For minority leaders, we often operate first as representatives of our communities—both in success and in failure—and only tangentially as individuals. Stereotypes about how we behave will always dog us. How we adapt to these stereotypes varies in large and small ways. I have a black friend who always overtips at restaurants. I know a woman who insists on demonstrating her numerical prowess at every opportunity, determined to undercut the idea that women are bad at math. A Latino acquaintance who speaks fluent Spanish but won't in front of white colleagues. A gay friend who refuses to engage in idle discussions about how cute some guy may be. These minor rebellions against perceptions all have an origin story, a stray comment here, or a long-held trope.

As the leader of the Democrats in the Georgia House of

Representatives, my job was to fight the opposition—the Republicans. The most visible opportunity to do battle happened in the well, the microphone and podium at center stage of the legislature. If you've ever watched C-SPAN or *Mr. Smith Goes to Washington*, the speeches lambasting the other side happen in the well.

When I became the minority leader, a.k.a., the leader of the House Democrats, I was the first woman to ever have the job— Democrat or Republican. Also, I was the first African American to have the role in the larger body of the legislature. My colleagues had seen me debate in the years before I ran for the position of minority leader. They'd seen me take tough stances against Republicans, deconstructing their arguments and facing volleys of questions from the floor.

But the instant I assumed a leadership role, perceptions and expectations changed. For more than 130 years, Democrats had ruled the legislature, which meant most of the minority leaders had been white Republican men. Sometimes outnumbered three to one, they'd used a strategy of confrontation and disruption to challenge the dominance of the Democratic Party. In 2004, after Democrats lost complete power in the House, following earlier losses in other areas of government, the new minority leader was, for the first time, a Democrat who days before had been second in line for leadership. But still a white guy.

My immediate predecessor, Minority Leader DuBose Porter, had paid attention to the way the GOP had fought him when Democrats were in power and he'd been the majority leader. Like any good pol, when the tables turned, he adapted and began to use similar tactics, railing against the Republicans' actions in front of television cameras, denouncing in loud and dramatic ways the excesses of their policies from the floor of the House.

Time and again, he would go down to the well and offer damning critiques, in a sometimes raucous show to demonstrate the insurgency of the Democrats.

Yet, when I became minority leader, I carried with me not only the legacy of what every previous leader had done but dimensions of difference that were patently obvious. As a woman, would I be seen as loud or shrill? As a black person, too assertive or aggressive? Worse, as a natural introvert, would my quieter persona be seen as thoughtful or weak?

As the first of my kind, I had no road map in the legislature to guide how I engaged these variables. For example, I am not a yelling politician, first, because that's not my style, and second, because stereotypes of African Americans and of women constantly hover over me. Not to mention the horrific caricatures of black women, who are denied both femininity and agency if we fall outside certain expectations. If I had taken to the well or to my new role by mimicking the actions of my predecessors, I no doubt would have become the "Shanaynay" of politics. Talk about stereotypes.

Instead, I carefully considered how I would approach my new role. I couldn't change superficial expectations, but I could, over time, alter perceptions. I spent time thinking about how I wanted to be viewed by my colleagues, by the Republican leadership, and by the general public. I also had to grapple with how my refusal to operate in the expected way would undercut my authority. Being aggressive in front of reporters could guarantee a great headline, but at what cost to the next skirmish? How would these mostly white men feel about being lambasted by a black woman?

These types of considerations never find their way into handbooks about leadership. But if I'd refused to think about them, I would have been an immediate failure as a leader. My job wasn't simply to fight with the GOP; I also had to negotiate with them to secure budget items for legislators' communities or good committee assignments. A slight they might have accepted from someone who looked like them became a stick of unstable dynamite in my hands. I'd seen how Speaker Nancy Pelosi morphed overnight from a shrewd, savvy politician to just a shrew in the characterizations of her opponents.

In the same breath, though, I had to signal to women, to people of color, to Democrats depending on me that I was able to represent and lead them. Stereotypes shape society's expectations for communities, as well as individual behaviors. By taking on the role of leader, I inherited the obligation to speak truth to power. If I cowered rather than roared, my colleagues would assume I wasn't equal to the task.

So I did the math. If I alienated the opposition by trying to behave the way men did, I would lose. Instead, I forced myself to look past my fear of disappointing my colleagues by not giving them the show they thought they'd see. I relied instead on my years of experience, where my personal style had prevailed. Pinnacles of leadership do not often occur without smaller moments of authority preceding them. As I examined my past roles, chairing committees and boards, even the days before I got elected as minority leader, I realized that I had already tested my theories on different stages. The fear that outweighed stereotype threat and authenticity conundrum was fear of failure: I had to be good at this, and I was best at being me—with minor modifications.

So I decided to disappoint Democratic expectations, but with deliberate care. Not unexpectedly, I found myself immediately criticized by my colleagues for not being more voluble and visibly indignant. To counter their disappointment, I sparingly issued press releases with stinging rhetoric, and their rarity meant the statements had greater effect. My speeches from the well had moments of high drama, but I leaned more intentionally on word-smithing and incisiveness than volume. And I knew I was a hell of a debater.

Under the rules of the House, the person giving a speech from the well can stand for questions or say his piece and sit down, unchallenged. One tactical advantage I discovered was that most of my colleagues did *not* like to answer questions from the well. I did. So, instead of yelling and gesticulating wildly, I learned to use my demeanor to my advantage. I gained a reputation for being effective in the well, for dismantling arguments and asking tough questions—from both Democrats *and* reluctant Republicans. I confronted the expected stereotypes by knowing what they were and building an alternate narrative about myself.

The reality, however, is that I am still critiqued as cold and aloof, whereas among my white or male counterparts, the same qualities are seen as being composed and introspective. In my campaign for governor of Georgia, former colleagues have questioned how "black" I truly am because I did not take on certain issues or do more to disrupt the normal order.

These critiques can be nullifying, eating at the core of who I am. More than once, I have found myself wondering if I have overcorrected, moving from one stereotype to another: from Shanaynay to Uncle Tom. When these doubts arise, my instinct is to quash them and bask in the righteousness of my decisions. I refused to be a stereotype, to be reduced to the memes of my community. But to defeat those labels and emerge authentic, we cannot simply ignore the fear of being treated as a single representation. We must examine our actions to ensure that our reactions are genuine and not a fear-driven response. Fear of being seen as too colored, as too female, as too much of what we are. The analysis must be internal, exhaustive, and honest. And, in the end, if you think you were right to behave as you did, then own it and move on. But do not avoid the internal investigation, however painful it might be.

Turns out, I don't worry if I am black enough or feminine enough much anymore. I spend time knowing my intentions, understanding my methods, and, most important, evaluating the results. There are times when I am more dramatic and incendiary (in controlled, well-thought-out bursts) and times when I hang back. As a leader, I have learned to be more accessible, not because that's the feminine thing to do but because it is more effective, and I watched smart women leaders who learned how to do so authentically.

The key is to find the balance between fitting in and being authentic. And this can be a constant battle—and understandably so. Even in 2017, examples abound: the young Latino man at a job interview who uses the wrong lingo is dismissed as "street" or uncouth, where the young white man is simply being "cool"; a woman who is boldly assertive becomes cast as the "bitch" in the office, losing out to the man whose behavior is lauded as "authoritative"; the black woman who wears natural hair in a space where being "too ethnic" is legal grounds for termination; or the Muslim woman whose hijab too often seems to the ignorant like an affront to what it means to be American.

Embracing your authentic self means being clear about how you wish to be seen. This doesn't mean feigning a personality that is artificial and then cutting loose at home. It means bringing forth who we really are while being acutely aware of our surroundings. From the moment I enter a room, I am clear about how I intend to be treated and how I intend to engage. I do not tell self-deprecating jokes about my race or gender, though I will do so about my personal idiosyncrasies. I can be charmingly humble or playfully self-effacing without pandering to stereotypes in order to make others comfortable. For example, my attire, my hairstyle, even my presentation style, reflect me rather than aping the behavior of others.

I know that when I offer criticism of men in the workplace, I may be seen as a man-hater. I know because I am not married, I may be seen as a lesbian. I know because I will never be less than curvaceous and wear my hair natural rather than pressed, I may be seen as sloppy or unkempt. The plague of the stereotype becomes the reason others cannot imagine how minorities such as myself fit into an organization or a role like governor of Georgia. So, instead, I can call attention to how my differences have prepared me to understand all the single ladies, the plus-sizes, and the folks who do not see themselves when they look at everyone else running for high office. I figure, why not give it a try?

My older sister, Andrea, is a college professor who teaches anthropology. One of a handful of tenured professors of color at her school, she found herself shying away from appointments to boards or committees. When she eventually conceded and joined them, one of her fears became a reality: every one of her comments, she felt, had to be profound, and she thought she couldn't make any mistakes. She saw herself increasingly held to a higher standard than her white colleagues and the pressure became intense. Although she wanted to start declining invitations, she stopped herself. As we talked, she admitted her worry. "If I don't do it, no one will. Then we're all in trouble." So instead, she has found ways to add other nontraditional voices to the conversations, choosing judiciously when she'll act or encourage others to do so.

Achieving too much creates the responsibility to be the spokesperson for all the people of color or all the women or all of any minority group who aren't regularly at the table. Being a token is real, and sometimes the urge to take a backseat so we don't have to be "the one" is tempting. But denying fear of disappointing everyone to avoid responsibility for everyone doesn't do anyone any good either.

Part of the job of leaders is to show why difference doesn't have to be a barrier. My colleague Simone Bell held the distinction of being the first openly African American lesbian elected to a state legislature. Simone joined a southern legislature that had awkwardly grappled with its first white lesbian ten years before, but mixing stereotypes of gender and sexual orientation with race proved too much for some veterans in the House. One member, a Democratic ally, urged me to tell Simone not to mention her status so often. It was making members uncomfortable. But for Simone, not only was her sexual orientation essential to her identity, it was central to her reason for running for office. She won her seat not because of her sexual orientation but because of what it signaled to an economically depressed, largely black community. Here was a woman who understood hardship and who had fought against the very oppressions that seemed to seethe unchecked in their communities.

Simone entered the legislature, ready to be a voice for mark-

edly different communities with a common issue of marginaliza-
tion. Quickly, though, she found herself the spokesperson for a
range of issues: AIDS funding, discrimination against LGBTQ
youth, and same-sex marriage. Simultaneously, her legislative district reeled from the Great Recession, and they clamored for her
response to slow action to revitalize their communities.

Among our colleagues, however, her sexual orientation
became the lens through which she was most often viewed,
undermining her effectiveness. Simone had every right to close
herself off from those who would reduce her life experiences to
a single story. Instead, she refused to shy away from tough conversations about her sexuality and found artful ways to reorient
discussions for broader meaning. When debates about public education came up, she used the experiences of bullied LGBTQ
youth to push for action against all bullying. Family leave debates
had an added dimension when she inveighed against the exclusion of same-sex families in workplace policies.

Still, she found that the constant machinations to be all to
everyone exhausted her and made her question whether being
in the legislature was worth the headaches. Her fear, she admitted, was that by being too much of everything, she was insuf-
ficiently focused on the core issues that led her to run.

Race and sexual orientation shared common threats, but not
identical ones, and when she stood too firmly on one side, she
stood accused of ignoring the other. I watched with admiration
as Simone came to the conclusion that the only way to conquer
the false equivalence was her active engagement, and she invited
those most discomfited to ask her direct questions. She acknowledged that race had complicated what they understood about
homosexuality, and she learned to welcome the inquiries. As she
told me once, the painful discussion had to happen if she wanted

legislators to know her and work with her on issues that she championed. Her cause was bigger than her fears.

Simone's experience also brought to light a common challenge among minorities: a competition for primacy of otherness. Fear points out not only the threats from the majority but our own actions that undercut advancement. For Simone, the choice was lesbian or black. Yet we know these parts of ourselves are so deeply intertwined as to be of a whole but experienced differently by those who may have only a single focus of otherness. Complexity in our identities creates strength, but we must guard against our own reaction to one another. We can overcorrect, like the Chinese American stockbroker who refuses to spend time with her Asian colleagues, for fear that she will be cast as just another minority and therefore miss out on a supportive environment and insight into promotion decisions. Or we sabotage one another, like the first-generation college grad when she mocks the outfit of a struggling student seeking an internship, cratering the student's opportunity to advance in order to prove her superiority. To a group, we are responsible for some of the maligning and undercutting. However, by confronting our own behaviors toward each other and our misguided expectations, we can tackle the fear and otherness that pit us against one another.

Fears about how our differences are perceived, about stereotypes that keep us back, about how our success begets more responsibility will never die. But once we are aware of them, we can work with them. Understanding how these fears guide our actions, even unconsciously, can point the way toward how to accept one's otherness but also accommodate the slow adoption rate of those we seek to lead. We don't ignore the fear of others. We under-stand it and harness it to our advantage.

Defeating fear of otherness means knowing who you are and what you're trying to accomplish and leveraging that otherness to our benefit. Knowing I'd never be invited into smoke-filled rooms or to the golf course, I instead requested individual meetings with political colleagues where I asked questions and learned about their interests, creating a similar sense of camaraderie. In business, I take full advantage of opportunities afforded to minorities but then always offer to share my learning with other groups that have similar needs—expanding the circle rather than closing myself off. Like most who are underestimated, I have learned to over-perform and find soft but key ways to take credit. Because, ultimately, leadership and power require the confidence to effectively wield both.

FIGHTING FEAR AND OTHERNESS

To confront our fears, we need to dive into how we think about
ourselves and our interactions.

Why I'm Awesome (Best Traits)	Examples of Trait in Action	Why I Admire This Trait

Why I'm Less Awesome (Worst Traits)	Examples of Trait in Action	Why I Dislike This Trait

What Others Say (Best Traits)	Examples of Trait in Action	Why They Admire This Trait

What Others Say (Worst Traits)	Examples of Trait in Action	Why They Dislike This Trait

Going Deeper

What are your core values?

What do you do for fun and why?

How do you make choices?

Who do you most admire and why?

Who do you most dislike and why?

What is your personal mantra? If you don't have one, make one up.

Three

HACKING AND OWNING OPPORTUNITY

In the winter of 2013, Georgia had more than eight hundred thousand unregistered people of color—a community the size of South Dakota who did not have the legal ability to vote despite being eligible. I sat in meeting after meeting where politicians discussed how distressed they were by the sheer number. Finally, I decided to launch a nonprofit voter registration effort to target these potential voters, whose decisions could shift the balance of power in the state if they participated en masse. I reached out to Lauren Groh-Wargo, a brilliant woman who had earlier helped me quickly train neophytes to become master campaign managers. I called and told her about my plan to register seventy-five thousand of the potential voters in 2014 and to get them all on the rolls by 2024. Lauren didn't hang up on me, to her credit. Instead, she and I began to plot our strategy. I would be our chief fundraiser, and to avoid any potential conflicts of interest, she would handle the actual processes so I couldn't be accused of bolstering

Democratic campaigns for House seats. Voter registration isn't partisan in Georgia, and while I can't deny I hoped every new voter would pick Democrats on the ballot, that wasn't my call.

Between March and August 2014, I raised more than $3.5 million, and we submitted more than eighty-six thousand applications to the state for processing. Which is when the New Georgia Project was placed under investigation by the secretary of state, who questioned how our organization could have registered so many people of color in such a short span of time without some misconduct. Yet, of the voter registration applications we submitted in 2014, an estimated forty thousand registrants were missing from the rolls on Election Day. For the next two years, my team and I would battle not only the accusations of the secretary of state, but also questions from our allies about what had transpired. Eventually, we proved the secretary of state had illegally canceled nearly thirty-five thousand registrations—including ours—and no wrongdoing had occurred on our side of the process. The secretary of state closed his investigation, admitting we had done nothing illegal. Better still, we've already registered more than two hundred thousand of our voters on the way to the full eight hundred thousand.

Still, the obstacles continue to pop up, as do questions about our success. For my efforts, I received a salary of $177,000—at or below the going rate for raising millions and registering tens of thousands. While a labor of love, running a massive operation that hired more than seven hundred staffers and covered the entire state of Georgia was a job. A wonderful, time-consuming, difficult job. Later, unattributed quotes in scathing articles decried my salary—criticisms I have never seen of men who accomplished far less and received outsize compensation. Despite posting the information on the New Georgia Project website, whispers continue to question our finances. The results should speak for themselves, but they do not always shout loud enough to drown out the objections. While the accusations sting, I wouldn't undo our work for anything. Opportunity is not synonymous with easy execution. Instead, it can be messy, tedious, and painful. I tell the story of the New Georgia Project because it gave me the opportunity to act boldly, to shift the political dynamics of Georgia, and to live my parents' teachings about civic responsibility. However, opportunity—including the chance to do good—is not a straight road, and to take full advantage, you must be prepared.

On the path to power—if you listen to the stories of self-made millionaires and political wunderkinds—the road to success has been laid out before us, with posted signs and rest stops, just awaiting our arrival. Go to school, study hard, get the right jobs, and the world will open its doors. The better narratives eschew formal education altogether. In these biographies, family garages become laboratories for genius. A loan of $10,000 morphs into billionaires' pocket change. Working up the ladder—corporate, political, or social—is not only doable, it is inevitable if you have put in the hours of effort. Do the right things and the gates will open.

The obstacles, we are taught, are merely challenges to be overcome by a combination of study, fortitude, and diligence. But the timely loan is rarely available in black and Latino communities where the average wealth is $7,500. Asian Americans do better, but the "model minority" stigma carries its own burdens, underestimating the challenges faced by those who live within the diversity of that community.

The myth of self-made success, or of bold action rewarded for its merits, may work in certain circles, but we're not often included in its penumbra. Self-made is a misnomer, a stand-in for a more complex narrative that includes the ability to work for no pay, to borrow from friends and family, to experiment and fail without falling too far. This is the comfort of starting on second or third base, thanks to the benefit of family wealth, or the presumption of qualification because of race or gender or background. Despite the American fascination with the gutsy move, society is more likely to punish rather than praise those of us whose performances stray from a prescribed plan. Consider the athlete who uses his platform to protest injustice, the woman who takes to social media to decry sexual assault, or the ex-felon who launches a business to give prisoners access to cheaper phone calls.

The space to invent ourselves, to reimagine *our* futures is narrower and sometimes seemingly nonexistent for those who do not occupy a place of privilege. Like everything else, to defeat the problem, we have to first deconstruct the fictions of golden opportunity and realize not all worlds operate the same. We assume if we work hard, plan well, and follow the rules, we will achieve great things. At the very least, the lore tells us financial comfort awaits. For many of you reading this, you know the truth is more complicated than the illusions fed to us by this narrative. We aren't going to win playing by the written rules. So we have to discover the hidden pathways to win. I call it "the hack"—by which I mean figuring out how to circumvent the traditional systems and own opportunity.

A good hacker acknowledges the innate impediments of the process. From early childhood, I watched my parents grapple in their different ways with the reality of this opportunity imbalance. My mom, who nearly dropped out of elementary school, clawed her way through the brokenness of divorced parents, unwed teenage sisters, daily hunger, and deprivation. She alone

of her seven siblings finished high school. As her class's valedictorian, Mom set her sights on college and never looked back.

My father became the first man in his family to attend college,
and what made his journey one for family storytelling is that he
is dyslexic. In segregated Mississippi, this condition was generally unknown, so his teachers often dismissed his different learning style as proof he was simply stupid. And back then, a black
boy who struggled to read certainly would find himself tethered
to the grim realities of life in the impoverished South.

Yet my parents, who met in high school, both made it to college and, as a married couple, they ventured north to Wisconsin
where my mom got her master's of library science from the
nation's premier institution for the subject. They stayed for a
while before returning to their home state, armed with the shields
of college degrees and advanced learning to ward off the plague
of economic uncertainty.

But as Mom and Dad and millions of folks learn in our country, a college degree is no guarantee of opportunity. Despite the
prestige of their educations, the "-isms" that stalk minorities do
not disappear when we cross the academic stage, and turning the
tassel from right to left isn't a magical ritual to open closed doors.
Doing exactly what we're told, amassing the education and the
accolades and the experiences, guarantees absolutely nothing. A
white family of median income sees a return of $55,869 from com-
pleting a four-year degree. A black family will earn a return on
investment of $4,846, slightly more than a Latino family at $4,191.

Mom got a job as a college librarian, where her paycheck
rarely reflected her worth. For my father, his struggle with
reading meant he took his bachelor's degree in history to a local
shipyard where he worked as a laborer for the next fifteen
years. Our family made the familiar journey of working class

to working poor and back again. Like the others who came before us and the millions to follow, college could not protect against economic anxiety. Still, we made it much further than those who dropped out of high school or who graduated and yet were unable to go further.

Growing up, not only did I see my parents struggle, I also watched them carve opportunities out of hardship. My dad took on odd jobs, cutting tree limbs and clearing lots. My mom used her research skills to consult for others, preparing background papers on an array of topics. They even ran a soul food restaurant for my great-aunt, an important lesson in the thin margins that operate the food service industry.

My parents never made it beyond the outer limits of the working poor—or lower middle class—but through their lives, I learned the beauty of human industry and creativity. Their story is just one of those I know. After all, we "others" often learn about the potential for fully realized mobility from the months allotted to us in the calendar: Black History Month (February), Women's History Month (March), Asian American and Pacific Islander Heritage Month (May), Hispanic Heritage Month (September–October). However segregated and relegated, these calendar-page-a-day stories tell an essential truth—that such mobility, such success, can be won by finding the point of entry to opportunity. Ida B. Wells used the power of her words to make real the sin of lynching for those who had ignored its horror, and in doing so, helped to launch a civil rights movement with the founding of the NAACP. Bella Abzug defied her party bosses to advocate for women, the poor, and the oppressed in New York, in Congress, and beyond. Linda Alvarado, a Latina woman, created one of the top-ranked construction firms in the nation and then bought herself a baseball team—the first Latino to do so. Tsuyako "Sox"

Kitashima lobbied Congress and won reparations for the victims of Japanese internment in America.

Once we understand our ambitions and learn how to admit and manage our fears, the next step is putting these lessons to work to find opportunity and own it. We will all, at some point, encounter hurdles to gaining access and entry, moving up and conquering self-doubt; but on the other side is the capacity to own opportunity and write our own story.

GAINING ACCESS AND ENTRY

The first impediment is usually access, making it tougher to identify where opportunities actually exist. Without access, we don't even know what is available. We are not members of the inner circle, where information is shared. Be it information or a skill set, denying access serves as a filter to screen out a lot of us before we know what's happened. Unpublished job openings, well-meaning warnings about being "enough" (smart enough, trained enough, tough enough), or unnecessary or unfair financial prerequisites can deter the most dogged go-getter. Confronting issues of access requires that you know where to look for the work-arounds or how to create your own. The second part, entry, means discovering the passwords to get inside.

Shiao is a young Chinese American woman who holds degrees in economics and Spanish. When she graduated from college, her professors encouraged her to go to work for a local chemical company that was eager to hire. She worked hard, learning the operations of the business, moving up the ranks slowly to a solid position in middle management as an expediter. But her heart has always called her in a different direction. Her goal is to work for an international aid organization, with a focus on Latin America, helping deliver supplies to needy communities. That's why she has maintained her Spanish proficiency, reading native language texts and participating in an online conversation group to keep her skills sharp.

However, Shiao lives in Indiana, and her only access to international organizations came through her college, now ten years in her rearview mirror. She faces a familiar obstacle to finding opportunity—knowing where to look and what to look for. Even after intense research on websites and job postings, she finds herself hesitating to act. She's never done this before, has only traveled outside the state once, when she did a mission trip to El Salvador. Despite the invitations to stay in touch, she failed to maintain contact with her hosts or the others who made the trip with her. Shaking off the worry that she's too late, she sends in application after application, receiving only silence in return.

Using these traditional methods, Shiao will likely never find a way into her new ambition. Soon, she'll convince herself to stay put at her day job. Sure, she is a fluent Spanish speaker who has the skills for the task, but she doesn't have the experience or the networks. After too many roadblocks, she'll quietly abandon her dreams and settle in to middle management at the chemical company.

Shiao's obstacles are not unique, but the tendency to pick those who remind us of ourselves and share our histories has high, devastating costs when your kind has rarely held power or position. Without anyone inside to give us access, we remain beyond the gates. For example, in the tech world, job hires are typically made through referral, despite the public posting of openings. By the time the posting makes the Web, a small cadre of insiders have already scheduled interviews and are picking out new ties for the first day of work. This tendency for like to hire like is not endemic to the environs of Silicon Valley—sadly, the cliché of the old boys' club is very much alive in the professional world. Name an industry, and if you peek inside, you'll find a list of go-to schools, a profile of the most likely hires, and hardly anyone in the upper ranks who looks like you. In politics, the hiring is public, of course, but to run for something often requires a toehold in the political establishment. If you look at elective office at the state level or mayors, in any state, they are more than 75 percent male and mostly white.

In the wake of the 2016 elections, dozens of groups sprang up to encourage marginalized communities to take action and run for office. These groups are perfect examples of uncommon points of access. Joining organizations such as Run for Something or Rise to Run, participants learn more about what's out there and who the gatekeepers are. Validators from within their ranks can offer lessons on how to plan a run for office or become a supporter. In the tech world, similar groups have formed to break through the clubby atmosphere of Silicon Valley. Lesbians Who Tech offers annual get-togethers around the country to discuss how their members made it inside—and they share how others can hack the process.

Shiao was right to try the traditional application process, but she also could have ventured the nontraditional at the same time. Submit the application, but then look for an unusual point of entry, like an alumnus of her college who had also gone into the foreign service. Regardless of the field, the degrees of separation are typically few (hence, the entire premise of LinkedIn). If you lack a direct route, like an application, try indirect options. For the more brazen, you can reach out to a current employee to seek advice. More than once, I've been contacted by job applicants who didn't wait for a call back. They were invariably polite but insistent, and I usually granted an interview, as a courtesy.

If a field has quotas, do not shy away from leveraging them as a way of getting started. Highlight your uniqueness and, during the process, offer examples of how this distinction can improve the organization. Quotas have long been both friend to and Achilles' heel for minorities. Without them, we find progress difficult, held back by the tendency of like to hire like. Yet, from affirmative action in education to hard quotas in organizations, the stigma of only being allowed inside *because of* difference yields a completely separate challenge. The quality of our work is questioned, our intellectual capacity doubted, and our success takes on the patina of illegitimacy. Defenders of academic affirmative action point to the prevalence of "legacy" admissions to counter this narrative, and I think they are on to something. Legacy is just another form of privilege, suggesting that close genetics signals qualifications. I have never heard of a student refusing admission to an Ivy League college because her father is why she got into the top-rated school. Likewise, we "others" must be bold in our acceptance of quotas as a way to advance.

When I became the Georgia House minority leader, I came face-to-face with a grim reality. Unlike the Republican majority, which had more than $1 million for staffing the committees and chairmen of the House, the Democrats received a paltry $13,000 for all our hiring needs. (To be fair, Democrats did the same to them.) My legislative campaign coffers had funds left over, so I transferred those dollars to the Democratic caucus I was set to lead. The next task required hiring staff with the limited funds available.

I began my project by doing as most do—hiring people I already knew. I didn't post the job descriptions or cast a wide net.

Instead, I picked a communications director who had worked for me on a project, then a chief of staff who had been on a campaign with me. I inherited a political director and an executive assistant from my predecessor, and I kept them in their posts. Looking around my newly assembled team, I caught myself. By only hiring those I knew, who had been picked by others who knew them, I wound up with a team that looked exactly like those who preceded me. Granted, my assembled team had an African American chief of staff, but every other staffer was white. Two were women but not the diverse team I frequently preached as the goal.

Taking myself to task, I reached out to the Latino and Asian American groups that had ties to political engagement. I'd already spent my entire allotted budget, plus my capital infusion, so the best I could offer were internships. One of my first respondents was Genny Castillo. She held a bachelor's degree in sociology and a master's in social service administration, and she was eager to enter the arena. Quickly, Genny became my go-to for constituent services, my coach when I needed to learn Spanish phrases, my innovator-in-residence when we decided to launch a statewide listening tour.

At the end of the legislative session and summer tour, Genny presented me with a brief on what she had accomplished and an assessment of what was missing in our structure. More impressively, she laid out why she was the person for the newly created role she envisioned. I was sold. I raised more money, and she became our caucus services director. In that role, she became a key resource for every Democratic representative in the Georgia House, expanding her influence and building her reputation. When I asked her to manage the nascent caucus internship program, as its inaugural member, she developed a program that has become a national model and has graduated more than 350 interns.

Every year now, we receive applications from across the country, and sometimes even international applicants jockey for spots.

Genny translated a nonpaid position into a full-time job, which also meant she had to have other part-time jobs. You may have to wait tables, work retail, or live with very understanding family or friends, but the benefits of internships are myriad: access to the industry, on-the-job training, and insider knowledge about what's expected. I promise, the long-term advantages are also worthwhile. Genny used her platform from the caucus to expand her other interests, developing skills across a range of areas. Her expertise in planning and logistics allowed her to launch her own consulting firm with my former chief of staff, and they now help candidates around the country and train political operatives of color to do what they've done. Genny began her role as an answer to a quota system but converted her access and entry into permanent opportunities.

Volunteering and internships are good avenues for finding opportunity, but sometimes it's sitting right in front of you and looks like grunt work or sloppy seconds. Don't be prideful. Be opportunistic. I have learned to watch for chances to act, particularly when no one else raises a hand. Sometimes no one volunteers because the job seems too insignificant. That's when real opportunity begins. It doesn't take much to polish a diamond, but turning coal into a shiny jewel is a surefire way to stand out.

Early in my career, our newly elected mayor of Atlanta placed me on a low-level task force to reform the fees charged for park cleanup—not exactly a sexy topic. Others at my level had been assigned to high-profile opportunities like ethics reform, infrastructure, or economic development, and here I was, working on trash fees. When our task force's assigned liaison, a white male attorney, drifted away from the project, I stepped in to lead the work and later presented our findings to the city council. The new city attorney was impressed by my innovative approach to a dull but thorny issue, and she later appointed me as the city's youngest deputy city attorney in its history. Opportunistic can mean opportunity.

MOVING ON UP

*O*nce we're inside, the barriers do not fall away. When we seek to enter spaces unused to our presence, the risk factor ratchets up exponentially. The demons of doubt may sound off in your brain, whispering about what could go wrong. Take too big a risk and you might lose what you have and not latch on to anything new. Tell too many folks, and someone might steal the dream out from under you. Hesitate and all is lost. Rivals and even well-meaning, protective allies can stand in the way. I'm thinking of the ones who urge against reaching too far because you do not meet every criterion or do not possess a perfect understanding of the role. I won't argue these are invalid worries, but they are necessary and manageable.

When I first decided to run for higher office in 2005, I vied for an open seat in the state House of Representatives. Eager to launch my campaign, I followed the traditional practice of seeking out endorsements from incumbents. I had given careful thought to my bid, and had written myself a memo outlining my personal SWOT analysis (strengths, weaknesses, opportunities, and threats). The SWOT analysis is typically used for business strategy, but I find it works just as well for personal review. On the strengths, I could list my tenure as a tax attorney with a specialty in health care, public finance, and nonprofits. As deputy city attorney for Atlanta, I had earned a reputation for being an effective analyst and voice for city operational issues. Add to that a range of awards and board memberships, and I thought I'd be a shoo-in. The legislators I had met during my time working for the city had often complimented my intellect and drive. Surely, they'd be pleased to welcome me into their ranks.

My qualifications were all well and good, but I had a host of weaknesses to address as well. Because I had never been much of a joiner, I hadn't attended the regular meetings held by the Democratic Party in my county, or even the ones held by the Atlanta Democrats. I had worked for politicians, but I knew very few of them personally. I had dismissed the relevance of building a social relationship with potential colleagues. As a result, they didn't know me and had no reason to help me out when I decided to run.

This weakness also revealed a key threat to my campaign. I could not rely on the anointment of those in power to serve as validators to potential voters. Endorsements are popular because they help convince voters they can trust you by showing who else does. However, with few formal endorsements, I had to find other ways to accomplish the same proof of viability. One of my strengths proved to be fund-raising. So instead of holding the money I'd raised for later in the campaign, I hired staff early on to help introduce me to the legislative district. A piece of mail would be thrown away, and television proved cost-prohibitive. Instead, I found local community members, introduced myself, and then hired them to knock on doors with me. In the end, I moved up, without using the same old ladder.

Beyond interning, one often overlooked hack for moving up is volunteering as a way to get inside an organization, then making the most of that position. I watched a young black man named Brandon Evans do this when I managed a friend's mayoral campaign. Brandon had a passion for politics, but he'd also dropped out of college during his senior year. Family financial pressures meant he could no longer pay tuition, and no number of side jobs could make up the difference. When the heated mayoral race began, Brandon reached out to a friend he heard was working on the campaign. The friend explained that hiring had been frozen, but he offered Brandon a volunteer role at the central office.

Brandon agreed to take the spot. His tasks were basic—collect signature sheets turned in by field staff, answer phones, and sign up walk-in volunteers. After a few weeks, he took his role a step further. He created a system of intake to streamline the process, began to organize the messy area where the field staff gathered and improved their deployment, and stayed late to close up the office. After a while, his improvements came to my attention. I reached out to him, asking about his interests. Soon, Brandon moved from volunteer to regional field director. After the campaign, he stayed in touch with me and his newly expanded network, gaining other political opportunities. Ten years later, he runs a statewide political apparatus.

By agreeing to volunteer, Brandon put himself in front of decision makers who otherwise may have ignored his application. More important, by doing more than the minimum, he made himself valuable to the team and distinct from other volunteers. While volunteer work can sometimes be a crapshoot and difficult for full-time workers, the ability to break through and move up is much stronger when those in charge can see your work with no risk to themselves.

Once you're inside, start to think about what's next, then take the time to understand the process for moving forward. No fairy godmother is likely to arrive to tap you on the shoulder. And believe me, the person next to you has also already begun to imagine the corner office. To develop the right connections, the most astute leaders look outside the C-suite. For those of us who do not have strong backers in upper echelons of power, unusual allies can be nearly as useful for identifying opportunities and navigating our way to progress.

One key approach is to cultivate relationships with those who have information and are typically ignored. For example, I am always genuinely engaged with support staff wherever I work. First, because these women and men too often work thankless jobs for demanding bosses and deserve our courtesy. Second, because they may be the only other minorities in the place, and it's nice to see a friendly face that looks like mine. Third, as I later learned due to points 1 and 2, it's the support staff who hears everything. A secretary who is asked to type a letter of resignation or an IT professional who overhears a story of company transition can be invaluable. What I have found is that these folks are often rooting for our success and will help circumvent the superstructures if you are open to their guidance.

I recently had lunch with a former head of diversity for a Fortune 500 company, seeking her support for my gubernatorial campaign. Before a few months prior, I'd never heard of Johnnie Booker. Having been connected by a mutual friend, we sat down at a table overlooking the Atlanta skyline, and I asked her about her path to her powerful role at the company. She gave me a sly smile, explaining she had taken a very circuitous route from her beginnings in rural Georgia, in a tiny rail-stop town. Over the next hour, I learned I was having lunch with a black Mata Hari of corporate intrigue. This matron, en route to visit her son and grandson in the Northeast, had once been among the most powerful women in American finance, but scarcely anyone knew it. Her secret, Johnnie told me, had been the secretaries and custodians in the offices where she built her empires. They would pass along memos left lying about, share secrets overheard in open corridors by men emptying the trash. With their intel, she carved out a space in the organization where she commanded millions of dollars—more than any person of color in her area—and created a program that lasted through multiple regime changes. She also had an early warning system to let her know when the men in her organization became rankled by her success. By knowing their concerns, she couldn't be ambushed in meetings or blindsided by evaluations. Instead, she climbed higher, leveraged her positions to take on new roles, and always brought others along with her.

Johnnie understood the power of the invisible workers, those whose knowledge may sometimes exceed that of the boss with the massive paycheck. To do their work, support staff must invariably learn the contours of their managers' jobs. They are the first eyes on calendar dates, the fingers typing up internal missives about next steps. They also hear about how you are viewed within the ranks of the company or organization, from bottom to top.

During my first year as Georgia House minority leader, I found out how critical this type of insight can be. As a new leader, responsible for guiding the actions of legislators who'd been in office for decades, I took seriously my responsibility to set the direction of the caucus's strategy. I consulted more seasoned members of the legislature as well as my predecessor in office. But it was Kay, the executive assistant whom I had inherited from the previous leader, who gave me the most important counsel.

She'd been listening for several weeks to the chatter among my colleagues. Uniformly, they acknowledged my legal acumen and ability to manage that portion of the job. What rankled them, however, was my behavior on the floor of the House chamber. If you ever watch C-SPAN, you'll note the flurry of activity when they cover the legislative process: empty seats with politicians chatting in small groups, whispering over desks, wandering around the floor. When others did so at the Georgia House, I remained in my seat, poring over the bills likely to come up or reading some report that could prove relevant. Where I saw myself as industrious, my colleagues saw distance and aloofness.

Yet, when I would ask for critical feedback, no one ever pointed out this concern. But they happily came to our office, sat in the comfortable chairs in front of Ms. Kay, and discussed this aspect of my approach. Lucky for me, Kay shared this information with me before the next election for minority leader. I never fully adapted to the etiquette of the floor, but I developed alternative approaches to build camaraderie. Sometimes, owning opportunity is not about progress—it's about not losing your place. Had I not learned to modify my behavior with her warning, I would have likely lost out to an opponent. Getting inside is part of the battle, but moving up takes constant care and feeding.

TAMING SELF-DOUBT

Sometimes, the hurdle to owning opportunity is ourselves. In order to combat our own notions of what we can do, we often play down our capacities, thinking we are being humble, when humility has little to do with our hesitation. Or we pretend disinterest as a proxy for apprehension. Self-doubt is vicious and corrosive, transmitting internalized messages that say we lack something essential for true success. These messages can be tricky and subtle, and take the form of seemingly logical interior dialogues that convince us we're not enough, sometimes without our realizing we've talked ourselves out of even wanting to achieve.

Zerlina Maxwell, an accomplished black journalist, shared her concerns about the false trap of self-doubt, which can present itself as false humility. She said, "It's frustrating to realize we're taught to be humble in a way that men are not." Though she meant black women, her comment applies more broadly—to women, people of color, and those who do not come from privilege. We deflect praise, pretending we don't deserve it. Worse, we actually think we don't. Our deference becomes a method by which to dial back aspirations, and we belittle our accomplishments for fear that those around us will laugh at our dreams. Because sometimes they do. But using the excuse of being humble is really a way of giving in to that laughter. It is self-doubt, plain and simple.

Too many of us, paradoxically, use the illusion of humbleness to keep ourselves down. The truth is that what we may think of as humility often disguises an embarrassment about ambition and a lack of self-confidence. We avoid taking advantage of opportunities because we wrongly believe that type of success is not for us. Real humility says, "I want something, but I don't believe that makes me better than someone else." Anything else is self-doubt displayed as self-effacement and signals, "I don't believe I'm equal to the other person who wants what I want."

In my early days in the legislature, colleagues would point out my grasp of a topic or a particularly good speech. Instinctively, I compared my credentials and my intentions to those around me and questioned their value. When someone would pay me a compliment, I deflected. My response typically consisted of a quick thanks, and then some variation of "anyone could do it." One day, a veteran woman legislator pulled me aside. "You need to stop giving your power away," she warned me bluntly. I asked what she meant, and she replied, "If these men think you're smarter than they are, let them. That means they'll come to you for advice, and you can help. But it also means they might follow your lead. But if you keep saying you're nothing special, they'll start to believe you."

We permit self-doubt to encourage us to downgrade our accomplishments before someone else does or in an effort to make others more comfortable with our newfound position or success. As we tell the revised story, our victory is rooted in circumstances, luck, affirmative action, you name it—anything but our own talents and abilities. This attribution to outside forces is very dangerous because if we didn't earn our achievement, then we can't replicate it. And we're less likely to take the next step and reach beyond our supposed limitations. Like the representative warned me, because our successes are not our own, they become vulnerable to erasure. Our earned victories are snatched away tomorrow, like a beauty contestant losing a title.

Real humility, on the other hand, is a deep anchor that connects us to our sense of self and pushes us to try more, try harder. Real humility says that we are grateful for the opportunities we've had. And we've also done our best to make the most of each moment, accomplished a lot, and will continue to do so.

Owning opportunity can feel like standing on a rickety ladder reaching for something on a higher shelf, knowing all along that, with one wrong move, everything could fall. Our ladders feel unstable because we've often built them ourselves from parts left lying around, constructed of other people's stories that are not like our own. Because we have never seen the job done by someone like us, we're not exactly sure what success looks like. In politics, I often find myself reading biographies of old white men, hoping to glean some wisdom that can help me figure out my next steps because of the paucity of stories about black women, women in general, or minorities of any kind. But the same is true in every sector. We are cobbling together a picture of what we want from a collage of faces and experiences that we don't recognize.

When we doubt ourselves into inaction, that paralysis becomes a habit. Rejecting opportunity is on autopilot, as familiar as our good-but-never-great self-narratives. So we tend to stand still and watch others achieve what we could have. A colleague gets your promotion. A rival pitches the book you always meant to write. A friend achieves her dreams, while you stew in a cauldron of safety, disbelief, and hesitation.

Angelica holds a degree from a prestigious college, and she works as the chief administrative assistant at a local food bank. She initially accepted the post out of necessity during a tight labor market, where jobs were hard to come by. Her graduation from college had been difficult, more "thank you lordy" than "magna cum laude." Over the years, she has been the assistant to a series of CEOs, each of whom marveled at her command of details, her organizational skills, and her compassion for their clients. More than one has suggested she apply for a different position within the organization, bringing her talents to a broader audience. Angelica longs to do more, to vie for one of the post openings. Every time, though, Angelica demurs. In the beginning, she doubted her capacity to take on a managerial role because of her poor academic performance. Years later, she has cemented her view of herself as a really good administrative assistant, one without any real special talents, yoked by an earlier stumble to a persistent stasis. Self-doubt has morphed from being a security blanket into a straitjacket for her ambitions.

Recently, Angelica joined a running group training for a marathon. Though she's run for fun, she has never seen herself as a marathoner. During their training runs, the women swapped stories, and Angelica mentioned a new opening at the food bank to be a team lead. When her running partner asked if she'd applied, she gave her normal excuses. She liked her role, it suited her. Another runner pushed her response and asked if she really had no interest. She pointed out that Angelica was the one who helped develop the training regimen for the runners, and how she had instinctively organized the running groups to match and strengthen the skills of each one. Over the next few sessions, Angelica shared more about her hesitations. Several conversations and miles later, at her friends' urging, she finally applied for the position and got it.

One curative for the voice of self-doubt is a louder chorus to drown us in praise, encouragement, and support. By opening herself to dialogue, and with a willingness to be honest about her concerns, Angelica invited a counterpoint to her own harsh self-critique. Talking to friends and close colleagues about aspirations and goals often exposes hidden doubts that hold us back.

OWNING OPPORTUNITY

Regardless of how we get in the door or up the ladder, we can never forget that the expectations for us are not the same. For women and people of color, the notion of a double standard is constant. For women of color, triple standards abound. Getting inside obliges us to increase our efforts, even when we are tempted to coast on our successes. Opportunity places even the most successful minorities between a rock and a hard place—trying to manifest the traits to signal we are qualified and have a right to be present while also holding fast to the qualities that got us inside in the first place.

Holding opportunity means learning how to position ourselves to constantly rebut the soft prejudices held against us. No matter how else "they" do it, we are often required to be credentialed. Whether the bona fides come in the form of advanced education, respected training courses, or job titles, be prepared to show your credentials. This is not to say you must have identical résumés to the insiders, but, if not, know how to explain yours and do not be surprised if a master's degree from your alma mater does not equate to a bachelor's from a colleague's school. Understand which degrees—and schools—are held up as models, and be brutally honest with yourself about where your credentials fall on the continuum. If you fall short, do not panic or abandon your progress. The obligation then is to anticipate the discrimination and be ready to demonstrate how you have effectively leveraged what you've accomplished.

That is, bolster your credentials with accolades. Here, the trick is to know what they mean and which ones you should take seriously. Having a litany of plaudits from unrecognized sources holds precious little currency. For example, getting a certificate of participation should not be on your résumé unless a national organization issued it to you. Instead, be intentional about serving because you want to do well or do good, but do not recite every honor badge you received. Become an effective critic of your accolades, or ask a trusted friend who has a sharp eye to be your opportunity wingman.

Beyond the paper endorsements, real live validators are the most critical prospects for advancement. Be certain others are willing to sing your praises—to you and others. These hype men and women serve as necessary reminders of your capacity for more, and their chorus of cheers will often generate an energy for change buried beneath fear of disappointment. We often underestimate the necessity of a friendly voice singing our praises. One of my favorite lines of poetry comes from Robert Burns: "O wad some Pow'r the giftie gie us / To see oursels as others see us." I have always translated his Scottish brogue to mean that we often miss the truths about ourselves—for good or ill—because we are blinded by our own internalized biases. In other words, "what awesome gift God could give us to see ourselves as others see us." For that reason, I have a regular habit of asking a small group of trusted friends to perform an informal 360-degree evaluation of me. Because each knows me in a different way, I learn more about how I am viewed in separate facets of my life. A word of warning, though. Brutal honesty is not for everyone. Still, having occasional insight is essential to self-improvement and to progress.

Of course, you also want to be certain these folks will tell others about you, particularly if they are sitting in rooms to which you have not yet gained entry. These supporters can explain you to the powers that be. Like the anger translator on *Key and Peele*, these advocates act as interpreters for those grappling with the distinctions made manifest by race and gender, age and class, and other traits that are neither white nor male.

Sometimes, we inadvertently constrict the aspirations of those who share our particular strain of otherness. Finding and owning opportunity is bigger than just us, bigger than our feelings of fear, and bigger than our triumphs. We need to be in it for others like us. Not only is this true, but acknowledging a broader responsibility can give us the courage to take a chance, and help us find bravery we might not otherwise have. To put it another way, diving in can be easier when you're saving someone else rather than jumping for yourself alone.

The imperative of showing it can be done is only logical. When no one in a poor neighborhood owns a business, the idea of entrepreneurship scarcely takes root. Kids who have never met a college graduate tend not to pursue higher education. Groups like EMILY's List and Higher Heights for America know that to convince women to run for office, especially women of color, you must tell them about other women who have run for office in the past, even if they haven't actually won. The pithy saying goes, "You cannot be what you cannot see."

In the end, finding and owning opportunity takes an intentionality that goes beyond showing up to work and doing a good job. The mantra is real: we must work twice as hard to get half as far. The fears that held us back return in force, undermining our forward movement, regardless of where we stand. We are, by our natures, often required to manufacture our own breaks, identify new openings even before others know they exist. The best hack is to know this is the case, accept it, and move on, prepared to take full advantage. And then do it all over again.

SWOT ANALYSIS: STRENGTHS, WEAKNESSES, OPPORTUNITIES, AND THREATS

This exercise will help you identify your personal strengths and weaknesses as well as focusing your attention on opportunities and threats to your development. The SWOT analysis can be performed using a variety of lenses, from noting external opportunities and threats in your professional life to those in personal relationships.

Strengths What are you best at in this environment? What are your finest attributes?	Weaknesses What are your areas of growth? What causes you worry about yourself?
Opportunities What actions can you take to improve your environment?	Threats What could impede your progress or cause you harm in this endeavor?

Four

THE MYTH OF MENTORS

At the age of twenty-nine, I became deputy city attorney for Atlanta, responsible for managing a group of attorneys at city hall. This despite the fact that I had never managed more than a handful of Spelman College Student Government Association members. The day I joined the team, I was the youngest member of the law department and, I soon realized, one of the most despised. The animosity wasn't hard to understand: I was an outsider, from a big corporate law firm, coming into a tight-knit group. To add insult to injury, I apparently got the job one of the most seasoned attorneys there thought would be his. My assigned team of attorneys did not like me, and they didn't mind telling me so. Every day, I sat in my purloined office on the third floor (which I soon discovered also belonged to the attorney who didn't get the job), surrounded by subordinates who seemed eager for my failure.

I spent weeks trying to win their support, holding meeting

after meeting where I tried to emulate every business leadership book I could find, only to be met with icy silence or condescension. Shifting strategies, I made plum assignments to those who seemed least likely to quit. Unfortunately, their colleagues saw this as me picking favorites, and the iciness became open hostility.

To be completely honest, I helped their hatred along by making missteps. Eager to prove I knew my stuff, I came across as arrogant. Not used to management, I valued substance over style, giving out assignments but rarely engaging in social conversation, coming across as brash and unfriendly.

One day I shuffled down to the second floor, to the office of Laurette Woods, the law department's financial manager, where she oversaw the department's budget and signed off on major purchases. I needed approval to buy a new computer, upon which I imagined I would eventually type my letter of resignation. Apparently, my depression showed. Laurette, who had also been trained in human resources, asked me what was wrong. I lied, pretending I had the situation well in hand. She waited patiently, processing my request, quietly probing for more details. Finally, I broke down and shared my frustration with the team and with myself.

Laurette offered me bits of advice: ways to establish my leadership, deliver hard assignments, and soften my personal touch. I complained, for example, about my staff meetings. I held my weekly staff meeting right after my weekly meeting with the city attorney. The timing, when I chose it, seemed to make sense, as it allowed me to stack meetings and move quickly from receiving instruction to delivering assignments. Invariably, by the time I made it from the city attorney's office down the hall to the conference room, two of my more recalcitrant attorneys sat at either end of the table, the rest of the staff arrayed around them. I had to hunt for an open chair and try to ignore their smirks. This petty power move worked each week, forcing me to the side of the table, mixed in with the other attorneys. They looked in charge, not I.

My options offered little hope. I could change the time of the meeting so I could get there first, which seemed lame. Or I could demand one of them move, which looked weak. Instead, I squeezed into whatever empty chair remained and tried to soldier through, the head of the table—the seats of power—occupied by infidels.

Laurette gave me a sympathetic nod, then her face grew serious. She said, "This is your team, Stacey, and you are in charge. So the head of the table is wherever you sit." Their pettiness only triumphed if I gave it agency, she advised. The physical seat had no power, and I merely fed their mutiny by playing their game. The next week, I excused myself from another meeting early, eager to get to the conference room before everyone else. I deliberately took a seat off center, where I could look around at my team. When the staff filed in, I greeted them with confidence. The rebels deflated as they entered, knowing I had changed the dynamic.

Over the next few months, I eagerly headed down to the second floor for my private tutorial on managing employees and learning to be a good boss. I made it a point to learn a new personal fact about each employee and to ask about their weekends before jumping into an assignment. Instead of summoning staff to my office, I would walk to theirs to connect. The first time I had to do a termination, Laurette role-played with me and taught me to not devolve into a debate about the merits. Once you've decided to fire someone, she warned, the kindest action is to be swift and final. Don't offer false hope or try to assuage your conscience. On this and so many items, she became a sounding board who showed me how to ask for help and admit ignorance. In turn, I have used her tutelage to guide others, sharing her insights and tips with those who find themselves without a Laurette to aid their journeys.

Yet, if asked who my mentors are, I do not automatically name Laurette. Not because she wasn't instrumental in saving my career, but because she's not who we are taught to see as mentors. In the law department hierarchy, I ranked higher than she. I never turned to her for legal advice, which was the crux of my position, so she did not provide subject matter expertise. And, on the face of it, Laurette was not responsible for my subsequent career moves into business and politics. I still wouldn't call her a mentor, but only because she is so much more than that to me.

Too often the idea of a mentor is a self-limiting device that has most of us hunting for someone we'll never find because of access or because our chosen guide already has a waiting list. Particularly if our target is the one woman who made it to the C-suite or the person of color who achieved success in our field, the reality is we're not the first to ask for help. By narrowing our sense of what a mentor can be, we ignore those who are all around, ready to help us hone our skills and build our leadership capacity.

I don't have traditional mentors. Instead, I have curated support, training, and advice from an array of alliances, advisers, and friends: an à la carte approach designed for maximum input and flexibility, for a range of circumstances that can defy the conventional wisdom of success. Minority leaders—like everyone in charge—need help and lots of it, from my experience. We need guidance, redirection, a sounding board, and correction. But we also have to learn to excavate our whole experience to find the right people to help us along. First, we have to under-stand what we're looking for—a counselor or a gatekeeper who sneaks us inside or a phone-a-friend who knows the right answers. Eventually, most of us will need all of the above. The trick is knowing what you need and making the right asks.

Then we have to be worth the time and effort required, which calls on us to do the hard work of being able to engage and sus-tain these vital relationships: to build real connections, construct broad networks, and learn how to be good at being helped.

Before looking for a mentor, you must first verify that you are a person worth the investment of time and energy you seek, which can be a daunting task. Be someone others want to see succeed by spending the time understanding who you are as a colleague or a boss. This personal introspection can be harrow-ing, as we all prefer to view ourselves in the best light. Yet, with-out knowing ourselves, we cannot fully appreciate how to seek support or to effectively use what might be offered.

I have taken more personality tests than anyone not currently browsing their way through BuzzFeed's ubiquitous quiz list. My Myers-Briggs type is INTJ, and I sit fairly equally in the four color quadrants with blue overtones. For communication styles, I am "high-touch" rather than more personally engaging, which means I forget to ask about your day but will go out of my way to figure out the system for arranging your carpool. We can argue the value of these analyses, but they tend to offer a fairly good overview of how we can be perceived by others. Aloof or overly social? Trustworthy but flighty? Well intentioned but unreliable? Self-awareness creates space for actually connecting with others in an authentic and sustainable manner.

Self-knowledge opens our capacity to receive support and to comprehend how we process advice and change. Beyond personality studies, review previous evaluations conducted about your behavior as an employee, as a boss, as a student. Note if the same descriptions consistently apply, or if areas of growth never seemed to improve. You can ask others for their thoughts on engagement with you, and if you monitor your reactions closely, you'll have a preview of your capacity to accept advice.

THE TAXONOMY OF MENTORSHIP

Business books and magazine articles extol the virtue of mentors without really explaining that the responsibility for the relationship is on the mentee. And a mentor is an attractive idea because, at its core, the relationship promises a certain degree of hand-holding as we traverse the complicated world of adulthood. For people of color, women, and those just starting out, in particular, there's a strong benefit to having a mentor to help navigate uncharted areas. If a mentor is what you want, then you must be clear about what you need. Often, for those who are asked to be mentors, the request sounds like a long-term relationship with multiple chances to be mutually disappointing. Like any relationship, the care and feeding of a mentor begins with understanding the rules—what to expect when you have a mentor.

Before diving into a mentor discussion, we should be certain we really want that level of advice and engagement. Clarity about why we call on certain folks can increase the value of the relationship and ensure its longevity. Sometimes, we are looking for a partner with more experience who holds a consistent position in our careers.

More often, though, what we need is less long-term and

more situational. I am a strong proponent of the situational mentor—a person who serves a temporary role or has a specific function, like helping negotiate salary increases or promotions. An additional dimension for minorities is that this can mean finding two or more for a single issue because navigating the challenges of diversity requires having an ally who understands intimately what we face, but we also need supporters who know what the majority thinks. If both can be found in one person, congratulations. If not, this is also fine. Changing who we turn to for advice will always be appropriate, as long as the choices are intentional and respectful.

Another type of mentor is the sponsor, the person who speaks up for you and helps open doors. Getting started in our careers, regardless of area of expertise, often proves the most difficult task, since the gates to opportunity are typically guarded by those who only allow those they know inside. When we have no historical claim to entry, a sponsor can be the proverbial key. A sponsor identifies opportunities that may escape our attention, vouches for our bona fides, and advises us on how to leverage the moment. When you're ready to move up the ladder or change careers, the sponsor can vouch for you.

As an economics major and college journalist, Raheem quickly distinguished himself as one to watch. He got good grades, was an active volunteer, and secured sought-after internships. When he landed his first job as a staff writer for an online magazine, he soon noticed a pattern. The bulk of his reporting covered low-income communities like the one he'd grown up in. Or he was tasked to cover beats with people of color. He applied repeatedly to expand into other areas of coverage, and he pitched solid ideas that became stories he did not get the option to write. At a loss, he asked the assignments editor to coffee. Raheem laid out his concerns and his body of work, particularly as compared to his peers who were progressing faster and getting the pieces they sought. David, the assignments editor, said he found Raheem's concerns compelling but demurred about whether anything could be done.

Discouraged, Raheem began to look for a new job, but he knew a transition would require a reference. He went to Sara, the section editor for whom he did most of his writing. He explained his discontentment and goal of leaving for another out-let. Sara expressed her surprise at his decision, and asked to see his portfolio. Rather than agree to serve as a recommender, Sara told Raheem to give her a few weeks to see if she could assist. At the next editors' meeting, Sara suggested Raheem as the writer for another editor, and extolled his consistent writing for her as well as how many ideas he'd pitched that had become sto-ries. The finance editor decided to give him an assignment, based on Sara's encouragement. Soon, Raheem started to get more varied assignments and eventually built a solid niche as a finance reporter.

As his sponsor, Sara opened a door for Raheem, and created accountability among the leadership at the publication. She had not been a constant adviser, but she used her position of access to create space for his success. To find a sponsor, look for the folks in the organization who have shown an interest—from hiring to assignments to more advanced colleagues on a similar path.

Similar but more intensive than the sponsor is the adviser, some-one interested and invested in your success but who has a deeper relationship, an advocate who looks out for your interests at a broader level. When I worked at the law firm, I faced a tough evaluation after my second year. I had been hired to be a tax attorney with a specialty in tax-exempt organizations, which meant most of my paying clients were nonprofit organizations. One of the reasons I chose my law firm was their solid commitment to the community, especially pro bono representation (working for free). Soon, partners in the firm were requesting my help with their pet projects, civic organizations where they volunteered their time—and soon mine. I loved these opportunities, but the time spent reviewing bylaws, starting up organizations, or setting up funding mechanisms had a downside. I spent more time on pro bono projects than expected, and my billable hours reflected my lack of corporate clients.

Teresa Wynn Roseborough, the partner who'd challenged me to think more broadly about my political career, stood as my staunchest advocate at the firm. It helped that she served on the executive committee, which reviewed all associates and decided their fates. When I received a mixed review—praise for my work plus scolding for my excessive pro bono hours—I brought my concerns to her. I needed to understand how to express my frustration with the process. After all, most of the pro bono projects had come from partners at the firm, and as a second-year associate, I couldn't exactly say no to their requests. Teresa agreed to share my concerns with the leadership of the firm, but she also explained my culpability.

Since I was an attorney, the firm rightly expected me to manage my time and raise red flags about any assignments that deviated from our agreement for me to bill a certain number of hours. She warned me to speak up when I saw a problem, reminding me that I would always have the best information about what was happening to me. With her help, my review soon reflected my good work, and we developed a new protocol for the number of pro bono partner assignments I took and how they balanced with my billable hours.

Situational mentors provide specific types of advice rather than career-wide support. They simply know more than you do about a particular subject or have key insights for specific issues. They provide advice, serve as a sounding board, or help with a limited set of circumstances. Shirley Franklin, who served as mayor of Atlanta, has been instrumental in my development as a politician and an administrator. As deputy city attorney, I worked closely with her on a range of issues, from tackling homelessness to coordinating agreements with hostile groups. I respected her extremely limited and valuable time by only turning to her for specific advice, though the questions ranged across topics. Working for her, I learned how important it is to balance effective administration with clarity and vision. But I didn't rely on her to be the only person to help me know how to do these jobs. Carolyn Hugley, the whip of the House Democratic Caucus, the second in command, also shared strategies for negotiating difficult issues at the state level. She had learned to navigate men in power, foster compromises among warring factions, and she taught me how to engage the concerns of others without losing my ability to lead. Serving as second in command, she bore the responsibilities of leadership, often without the recognition of her brilliance, and from her, I gained a deeper understanding of the contours of true engagement.

Even my writing career has benefited from situational mentors, including people I've never met. When I launched my career as an author, I had never met a professional author. Most of my skills had been gained by reading really good writers. Aristotle's *Poetics* and Nora Roberts guided my earliest forays. Aristotle perfected structure, and Roberts understood how to marry suspense and romance in ways that didn't underestimate her audience. I wanted to be the kind of writer who wrote smart novels that people wanted to read and that had a romantic suspense element at their core, but which weren't diminished because of their genre. From Nora Roberts's writing, I learned how that could be done effectively. In real life, Pearl Cleage also taught me about how to write a killer novel. At the time, she was an award-winning playwright and nonfiction author, though she later wrote best-selling novels. I took playwriting from her at Spelman, where she taught about structure and story arc in ways I found to be invaluable in constructing novels and forging a new trail.

Peer mentorship comes from those who are similarly situated but may know something you don't. Especially if you're interning, take that opportunity to try to gather insights and advice, not only from the senior person but also from your fellow interns. We ignore peer mentorship to our detriment, but the mutual benefit outweighs any concerns, as these are often the allies who best understand your current circumstances.

Jess, a young white woman, is as savvy as they come. She's moved quickly up the career ladder as an engineer, and she has become a rising star on the management side of the building. But Jess is horrible at valuing her worth in a male-dominated industry. Every time she receives a promotion, she immediately accepts the salary offer, unaware of what her colleagues are receiving for the same work. No one in the company will tell her to ask for more money, and the culture of silence around perks and bonuses is complete. At a national networking event, Jess met Patrick, who had a similar role in a different company. Though they are competitors, Patrick, a young African American, faced a similar information vacuum.

Jess and Patrick began to commiserate and then realized they could help each other. They shared salary information and triangulated how well they were compensated. Jess called Patrick when her next bonus discussion came up, and they role-played how she could demand more. When Patrick heard about a new lateral position similar to Jess's role, he reached out to Jess to strategize about how to put himself in the running. Jess and Patrick live thousands of miles away from each other, and they are not close friends. But their shared experience creates a situational space for mutual support and advancement.

My own experience with a peer mentor led me to develop my business expertise. Lara Hodgson—my longtime business partner—and I joke that I got my MBA from working with her, and she is now a lawyer because of me. When I decided to run for office in 2005, I quit my job as deputy city attorney and started my own consulting firm. Reluctantly. I had no interest in being an entrepreneur because I liked paychecks. I liked having a steady workplace where I showed up and did my best and someone paid me for my efforts. I did not like the thought of being dependent on my own ingenuity to make my daily bread. But the urge to deepen my public service demanded that I abandon my stable public service post and become an entrepreneur—because no one else was going to hire someone who planned to be absent from the office for six months for a campaign.

So, I quit my job and had to make other arrangements. Instead of going to work each day, I decided to start a consulting firm that leveraged my experience in tax policy and government to help the city's largest public-private partnership get off the ground. I priced my services and pitched myself to Atlanta BeltLine, Inc., and they hired me. However, when I won my election, I could no longer rely on my single client to sustain my company.

Enter Lara. Lara worked for a major development firm as its chief operating officer, but she too was in the midst of transition. We began e-mailing and texting each other late at night, fantasizing about the company we wanted to start together, one that combined her private-sector experience and my public-sector know-how into an infrastructure consulting firm. I jokingly code-named our discussions "Insomnia" because of the three a.m. e-mails.

Lara, a Georgia Tech aerospace engineer and Harvard MBA, had already been part of the launch of several other companies, including a shoe firm backed by Shaquille O'Neal. Over the course of several months, we shifted our musings into plans and plans into execution. In 2007, we established Insomnia Consulting, LLC, and began to bring on clients. I watched Lara pitch our business and deftly explain how we could be a benefit to their established companies. Listening closely, I learned the language of the business world, first parroting her and then owning the new lexicon. We sat at her dining-room table and plotted how we would present our services to an array of Fortune 500 clients, and we critiqued each other—how to say this more effectively, how to frame that for easier consumption.

We began with Insomnia, then started Nourish, a manufacturing company, and our last start-up together was NOW Corp., a thriving financial services company. I never would have attempted such a variety of corporate endeavors were it not for Lara's mentorship. Although we were partners in our ventures, my relationship with Lara helped me immeasurably—and taught me skills that cross sectors. She advises, educates, and encourages, the best aspects of a mentor.

BUILDING NETWORKS DEEP AND WIDE

Cultivating relationships, alliances, and friendships as tools for effective leadership is a vital approach to growing our own capacity. Though for every minority in industries where there are fewer women, fewer people of color, fewer "others" of any kind, the challenge of finding a proper mentor—in any form—can overwhelm even the most confident.

To find a mentor who will be able to help guide you on your path, try both the traditional and the unexpected. Networking events or mixers are the most popular venues, and they provide contained spaces where you can connect and start to develop your board of advisers. Think about it like speed dating—the goal is to see if there's a spark, but you're not there to fall in love. You should use the conversation to gain basic information, share background details, and exchange contacts. If the connection feels right, then move to the next phase of the relationship, the coffee (or breakfast or lunch). This is the time to measure compatibility and decide what more you want from the relationship.

Within an organization, one of the best methods is to ask for an informational meeting. But either way, the initial conversation should largely focus on the mentor, not on spilling your guts or asking for help. This is a professional courtship, so ease into it. My business partner, Lara, is fearless about reaching out to those whose careers pique her interest; thus she has cultivated one of the broadest networks I've ever seen. She maintains quality relationships by calibrating her outreach based on the preferences of each person. In fact, we became friends and business partners because she heard me speak at an event, and she reached out to me to learn more. And a peer mentorship was born.

I came of age in a time before the formal discussions of mentorship were so ubiquitous, or perhaps they happened beyond my earshot. Knowing I had a varied set of interests and limited access to successful folks with my goals, I took a different route to tutelage and support. Instead of seeking out a single guide, I built my own informal team of coaches who possessed the skills or held the jobs I thought would be important for me to have. In politics, the first time I actually ran for office was for a post in student government. With that victory, I had a chance to get to know our college president, Dr. Johnnetta Cole, on a closer level. I remember sitting in the kitchen in the president's house, just listening to her and asking questions and learning about how she got to where she was and how she navigated the challenges of running that college.

While she ran a college and not a city, she had a set of experiences that I saw could improve my effectiveness. For example, working with Dr. Cole, I learned how to fund-raise. She allowed me to watch her make fund-raising calls and attend swanky events I'd never heard of. Not only did I see how she traversed a range of obstacles, I learned from her to be fearless in asking for money. She also sent me on my first informational interview as I tried to figure out my path. Despite my spreadsheet of milestones, I still had to get from step to step. I shared my ambitions with Dr. Cole, and she, in turn, identified leaders in nearly every sector for me to meet and query about their paths. Dr. Cole has never stood for public office, but from her, I became a better political leader.

I know that when you're the only woman of color in a space, not a lot of people are clamoring to be your mentor. Sometimes finding that person—or people, even—is very difficult to navigate. Building a mentorship network can be a solid alternative and a way to have the array of supporters you'll need: the sponsor, the situational mentor, and everything in between. To build this network, though, we have to adjust our expectations and be intentional about what we seek out. A good mentorship network has a number of advisers with specific profiles.

In your network, be certain to have an adviser who does not look like you, sound like you, or have your same experiences. A good adviser should offer a contrasting view because of gender differences, racial differences, socioeconomic background, and so on. We get stuck in our own heads, and an adviser who offers a starkly divergent personal history can sometimes illuminate what we miss in our own experiences. One of my closest confidants is a white guy from South Carolina who is also involved in politics. He has a sharp mind, asks incisive questions of me, and forces me to sift through the detritus of important decisions to focus on the main issues. Because of our real connection, I do the same for him, pushing back on his analysis and enlarging his understanding of a situation. Because we do not share identical life histories, his perspective gives me a window into how to filter discussions and sift through my own readings of events. I do not have to abandon the viewpoints informed by my life story, but I also have the additional capacity to integrate other angles and takeaways.

Add in someone who has skills you admire. That might be someone not in your division; it may even be someone not in your
field, but someone who has the ability to help you understand
how to navigate your field. A few years ago, I met a young woman
who trained as a lawyer, but she decided that she wanted to go
into education policy. She and a friend of hers came to see me at
the state capitol because they'd heard me speak at a conference
on education held by a black women's policy organization. When
I asked why they came to see me, both said there weren't black
women in their organization who had achieved high levels of
leadership, and they wanted to ask my advice on which skills had
moved me forward.

One of the young women, Tiffany, was incredibly shy—her
friend did all the talking—but I said to both of them, "If you want
to continue speaking with me about your careers, I'm happy to
help, just follow up with me." Her friend never reached out again,
but every three months, I hear from Tiffany and we have a skills
discussion. She quickly updates me on her progress, and she'll
usually have career questions for me that are clear and specific.
Sometimes, she presents a situation where she has to make a decision, and she wants my insights. Or she describes a peer encounter
where she questions her reactions. Most recently, we had a great
discussion about being effective in a meeting. She described a
series of meetings where she raised her hand and didn't get
called on but others did. Or where she made a statement and no
one paid attention, and then the guy next to her repeated the
exact same words and received applause. She wanted to understand how to deal with that situation, and we discussed ways to

inject herself more forcefully and to react in a productive manner to the oversights and slights.

I am not in her corporation, but the experiences that she's having are ones that happen to women no matter where you are. What I've been able to do is help her navigate those conversations and deepen her emotional IQ at work. I may not be in her field, but I've had that experience. She has a mentoring network that includes people like me, people who may not have exactly the background she has, or who do not want the same things that she wants, but are willing to help her be the best person she can be to achieve her goals.

HELP THEM HELP YOU

Building real connections that make up a broad network is most effective when you learn how to be helped. With the proliferation of the mentor myth, I find too many have false expectations of the relationship. More than once, I've been asked to be a mentor, as though there's some "mentor handbook" with a set of instructions. Worse, those who ask to be mentored tend to have only a vague notion of what they want. Fundamentally, the responsibility is on you, as the mentee, to create the mentorship that you want and manage expectations, especially your own. Each person in your network will have a personal style of engagement, and you should understand how to be easy to support.

Something I learned early on is if someone says, "I want to help you," believe her. I later understood what they mean is "Help me help you." Recognize that the person has a number of other holds on his time. Tiffany and I have a regular check-in every three months. She sets a time on my schedule, prepares her questions, and we chat for nearly an hour. This type of structure is not required, but it works for us. Of course, she can always contact me when a need arises; however, we have this formal ongoing check-in to provide structure and regularity. And do not wait for your mentor to reach out to you—that's your job. You don't want to be a stalker, but you want to be aggressive in your curiosity. Ask important questions that you need answers to that you can't find anywhere else. The corollary to that is not to ask questions just so you can sound like you have something to say.

Second, don't wait for them to offer aid. Ask for what you need. You are intimately involved in your daily life and aware of the complexity of your situation. No one else has that insight. Reach out when you must, and be prepared to connect the dots. Some people just like to complain and have someone listen. Thus, it is your responsibility to affirmatively ask for engagement and support. Do not drop hints—they'll lie on the ground forever. Do not anticipate the response, and give them a chance to help or decline, but don't decide for them. Do not extrapolate: a "no" or a failure to help on one issue should not lead to an existential crisis about the relationship. If your mentor has helped before but doesn't this time, ask why. The worst reaction is to spin out a false theory rather than gain useful information.

Third, become a mentor yourself. The best way to learn how to manage a good mentoring relationship is to be in one yourself. In every facet of my career, I've been privileged to offer those opportunities to young people. By working with Tiffany and others, I have developed a better sense of how to leverage those wonderful women and men who have helped me along the way.

Regardless of the type of mentor you're looking for, the hard work of understanding who to trust and how to grow relationships of substance changes how effective we are as leaders. This is a sorting process, forcing us to make difficult choices about who to befriend, and the reality is that not everyone is the right person upon whom to rely. In addition to personal insight, we must also be willing to give before we receive. People tend to help those who are open to helping others, not those who help themselves. Though this sounds overly simplistic, the harsh reality holds true—we need all the friends we can get, and the best way to gain support is to be supportive. One of my favorite sayings, which I learned from a long-serving member of the state legislature, is if you see a turtle sitting on a fence post, you know he didn't get there alone. Someone had to pick him up and put him there.

I would not be in the places I stand were it not for the women and men who helped me get there. Their support, while altruistic, came about in part because they trusted I would be reciprocal in my allegiances. Real connections grow out of shared moments, out of being able to ask for aid, and by asking, "How can I help you?"

But beware. Professional friendships should not be mistaken for slumber-party friends. Unless a clear transition from office to personal has occurred, effective relationships should respect boundaries. Sharing marital issues or family turmoil to create a sense of intimacy often backfires. Instead of baring your soul, the other person may interpret a lack of discernment or wonder about your decision-making skills. Professional friendships can also seem more transactional, but that's not always a bad thing. If you share a tip about an opportunity, saying "I may not be able to take advantage of this, but let me tell you about something I heard about," you create space for reciprocation. Offer feedback, such as "Let me tell you something that I saw you do that I thought was fantastic, and let me give you a little bit of advice about something that no one else is going to tell you."

This type of engagement helps build camaraderie and an internal connection for a longer-term relationship. Real connections exist when someone is willing to be honest with you, and the way you cultivate that is by being honest with them. Now, what I'm not saying is to go around telling people what's wrong with them. But always be prepared to ask, "How can I help?" In our campaign, as in my legislative office, a question we start with is "How can I help?" Sometimes, the way I can help is by admitting that I can't and finding someone who can. When you maintain relationships by trying to find ways to serve others, the effect ripples out. Generosity in our engagements transforms who we are and expands where we can go. Thinking this way about alliances can feel calculating—and it is. But the goal is to be a person folks want to help, and that is best achieved by being someone who sincerely lends a hand to others. Plus, the psychic benefits pay dividends. When we assist others, we get company up on that fence post. We lift up a young woman who sees something new in herself that she'd never recognized before. We become the sounding board for the colleague who calls to share a moment of panic: "Here's how I screwed up on Thursday, and I do not want to go back into that space. Can you help me think about how to do it?"

Then the days when you need that help, when you need to call and explain, "I said something stupid in a speech, and I need help to fix it," or "I probably screwed up the delivery schedule for the next decade," you have a sounding board ready and waiting.

I may have never had the mythical mentor, a career Sherpa who guides us through travails of professional life, but I have benefited from the array of women and men willing to share wisdom and cautionary tales, to redirect my path. Because my trajectory has included several distinct tracks, I rarely held a post long enough to cast a single figure as my mentor. My story is more like the "it takes a village" theory of support. The one-stop mentor typically is not a viable option for too many of us. For one, we probably will not be in the same place long enough to have a full-career guide. Then the issue of difference enters. Confronting the challenges of diversity with a true understanding of the role of mentorships will make the journey that much more doable. But the extra work is all worth it.

In 2017, I received an honorary degree from Spelman, and Dr. Cole flew in for that awards ceremony to surprise me. She spoke at the event, sharing her role in my eventual career choices. Even though she wasn't in politics, she helped me take those early steps. After all, she is the person who told me I complained too much and if I wanted to change things, I needed to do something about it and run for student government. Mainly I think she wanted me to stop bothering her, but look at me now.

BUILD AND EVALUATE YOUR BOARD OF ADVISERS

Understanding who you have in your corner can help you figure out who's missing.

- Sponsor: You have a cordial relationship but not a deep one. Speaks up for you and can open doors.

- Adviser: You have a more complex relationship. Offers more consistent advice and is engaged in your long-term plans.

- Situational: You know each other, but the core connection is the person's subject-matter expertise.

- Peer: Similar to you in age or position. Can offer insights and help game out situations.

Name	Type of Adviser	Area of Expertise

Five

MONEY MATTERS

My great-aunt Jeanette participated, almost religiously, in the Publishers Clearing House Sweepstakes. For years, she returned the subscription cards inside those brown envelopes with their Prize Patrol promises on the outside, certain that this time, Ed McMahon would come knocking on her screen door, balloons and oversize check in hand. As I sat with her, on a sunken couch covered by a handmade quilt, she'd tell me of the wonders wealth would bring. She'd buy everyone a new house, would finally visit Paris and the continent of Africa. An educated woman, one of the few of my relatives with a college education, she had never quite escaped the deprivation of her upbringing—instead, she'd simply moved down the street. But one day soon, she'd win $5,000 a week for life.

Brandy Clark, a brilliant country music artist, sings one of my favorite songs, "Pray to Jesus." In the lyrics, she writes of the relentlessness of the working-class economic struggle and the alchemy of escape, saying that the options are stark: hope for divine intervention or win the lottery. In Georgia, as in other states across the United States, politicians have harnessed this desperate belief, funding millions in education from the daily dreams of the scratch-off ticket and Powerball.

As ever, it remains true that in America, money dictates nearly every step of social mobility from our very first moments of life. Where I grew up in Mississippi, Pass Road Elementary School was the poor school, Anniston Avenue Elementary School had the middle-class kids, and Bayou View Elementary School hosted the rich kids. My parents made sure we lived on the poor street on the middle-class side of town so we could be zoned into Anniston, the good school, and even it wasn't quite good enough. Several times a month, a handful of us filed out to a short yellow school bus to travel across town to the best school. That's where QUEST, the city's gifted program, convened students, where the resources were plentiful and the bulk of the gifted kids studied every day. This level of economic cartography is far from unusual, and the correlation between wealth and academic achievement doesn't happen by accident. Educational access, like so much of society, is determined by zip code, meaning whether we live where property values soar or sink. The wealthier the area, the higher the returns. Those with means hire tutors for their kids and enroll them in enrichment courses or extracurricular lessons like piano or dance. The rest of us play public education roulette, hopefully landing in an adequately funded school with a sports team and a band. This matters, because education is one of the strongest predictors of economic success.

How much our parents make also often determines if we go to college and what kind. I recall scouring books in our high school library, hunting for scholarships (before the advent of the Internet).

Even as the school's valedictorian, the scrabble for money was real. I not only had to pay tuition but also housing, food, transportation, books, and a host of other costs I never contemplated. I entered the gates of Spelman armed with academic credentials and poor financial literacy. Unfortunately, although I graduated with studies that included economics, I still left college unaware of how my untutored financial missteps would haunt me for decades. Because money is more than the determinant of where we learn. Not understanding how financial decisions work becomes a millstone for our other ambitions, like whether we can afford to run for office or launch a business, or if the work we do will keep us bound to a job we hate because we can't afford to escape.

Money is one of the most impenetrable barriers because most of us start without it, and it stays that way for a while. For you and me, the disadvantages are real: we scrape together money to fund higher education, if we can attend at all. From making a deposit on a car or a down payment on a house, we may not have family resources to get us started, so we compromise or delay or simply give up. Whether we are dealing with personal finances, funding a campaign, starting a business, or leaving one opportunity for another, money can be a crippling obstacle to power and leadership. Not only do we lack the resources; women and people of color are typically viewed as beggars at the table, not the bankers behind the desk. This perception means that even when we are primed for access, our engagement with money is met with suspicion and false impediments. Worse, we self-destruct or at least hamstring our own promise. We make necessary short-term choices without full appreciation for consequences. Sometimes, we mistake income for wealth—not understanding the difference until too late.

One way this disparity plays out structurally is that as more minorities move into business ownership, the redlining of women and racial groups continues. Redlining began as a practice of cordoning off communities where lenders refused credit, often to deny people of color or other "undesirable" demographics the right to buy houses. Over time, though, redlining has become more sophisticated, extending beyond home purchases to other forms of credit. Denial of credit and lending creates barriers to entry that cannot be overcome with the usual prescriptions. The truth of the matter is that most of us do not have assets to borrow against or a trust fund to access—we have limited wealth. Even with that good-paying job—excellent income—we still live paycheck to paycheck for quite a while, rarely able to build wealth because we're paying for past mistakes.

The common solution I hear for those who are eager to excel, despite their lack of personal wealth, is to reach out to "friends and family" for help. But for those of us from families without means, the advice to borrow or raise money close to home is at best a cruel joke. Wealth gaps are staggeringly wide, and they concentrate in communities. If your community struggles, hope is not on the way.

But minority leaders find ways to thrive, and try we do. We just have to work both smarter and harder. We start businesses and focus like a laser on beating the odds. White women may have an advantage, as long as they stay in their competency lanes—focus on the areas women are good at, don't dare to venture into tech, construction, or manufacturing. For people of color, the disadvantages pile up regardless of area of expertise.

In politics, competent minority and female candidates may eschew running altogether or seek lower offices because fundraising can be daunting or even disqualifying. If successful, people of color often face questions about how they raised their money and if they are capable of properly spending the funds. Women and people of color find themselves accused more often of potential corruption driven by nothing more sinister than unexpected success.

Having faltered in several respects, I now approach the issue of money much as I do everything else: understand the issue and try to figure out how much I can do with what I've got. The first step, for everyone, is tackling the challenges of personal finances, from financial knowledge to creating personal security to building confidence with money, because with personal financial worry weighing us down, we often can't move on or up to more. Next, we must develop the skill of financial fluency, expanding our grasp of fiscal responsibility into the professional realm, where we're not usually expected to speak the language. Command of financial lingo and the dexterity to read and understand the spreadsheets and balance sheets behind institutions dramatically alters our authority and potential. Finally, when we master the art of raising money across the board, we are prepared to move from participant to leader. From the difficulty of borrowing money as an entrepreneur to fund-raising for nonprofits to raising dollars as a political candidate, conquering the complicated nature of money allows us to make different choices and expands how effectively we can gain power.

MONEY MISTAKES MATTER

In my first years out of law school, I found myself having a certain discussion with fellow attorneys, typically either the women or the people of color, again and again. After the heady experience of paying more in taxes than some of our families had earned in a year when we were growing up, the allure of money came into tension with the desire for a different life. They even have a term for it—"golden handcuffs." Getting used to the comfort of wealth (or its close approximation) makes choices and risk taking that much harder. Because risking something when you have everything to lose is real.

When I graduated from Yale Law School in 1999, the economy was booming. My initial job offer from the law firm where I interned proposed a stunning first-year salary of $75,000. Then a national salary war broke out among law firms, as they tried to outbid one another for the legal talent on offer. By the time I started my job—the same job that offered me $75,000 mere months before—I had a starting salary of $95,000, much more money than my parents made—combined. Plus, in corporate law firms, the starting salary came with an automatic increase each year.

My colleagues purchased luxury cars, bought houses, and took spur-of-the-moment vacations to Europe and islands I'd never heard of. Others dutifully socked away dollars into their 401(k)s. I made my own upgrades, trading in my 1994 Chevy Cavalier for a sleeker 2000 Chevy Cavalier. My apartment had two bedrooms instead of one, but I still rented. You see, even though I now earned nearly six figures, I had the credit rating of someone much poorer. I possibly could have qualified for reasonable financing for a Honda Accord, but I didn't chance it and no one was selling me a house.

During college, I had done what so many without money do. I used scholarships to cover the written cost of college—tuition, housing, and fees—but for everything else, I borrowed. Every credit card application sent to my PO box had been swiftly converted into magical slivers of plastic that allowed me to pay for the necessities of daily life. My parents had no capacity to support me financially. They were finishing up their own studies in graduate school, working full-time in jobs that barely kept their heads above water, and raising four kids still at home. My sister Andrea was entering her senior year at Agnes Scott College when I began at Spelman. My younger sister Leslie, two grades behind me, would be heading off to Brown University soon thereafter. No one in my family could afford the private colleges and universities we attended without the combination of academic scholarships and federally subsidized loans, Mom and Dad included. So we all borrowed heavily through financial aid and credit cards, and I earned extra money working during the summers and then in various jobs during school.

The problem was, though, I didn't have the financial literacy to understand the hole I was digging for myself. I hadn't learned much about money management ever. My parents taught me the value of education, the necessity of service, and the responsibility of keeping your word. However, I never saw them balance a checkbook, and I had no conception of the evil genius of the FICO score. Sure, when I could, I paid the bills that regularly arrived from the credit card companies; but soon, the amounts they wanted outstripped what I had left from that semester's loans. Loan proceeds paid for my phone bill and transportation and clothing, and everything left over went into the family pot—helping not only me but my family survive.

By the time I graduated from college, I owed tens of thousands in college loans and thousands more in credit card debt. But grad school immediately followed college, and with this extended education came the dubious ability to borrow even more. Tuition and fees were fully covered by fellowships; still, I had learned the art of deferred debt too well. Let's be clear—I wasn't spending money on spring break or other splurges. I lived modestly, first in dorms in college, then studio apartments in grad school and law school.

However, my family had expenses, and we all chipped in. My brother Richard had started college, and I diverted some of my temporary gain to him. (If you are counting, that's four kids in college or grad school at this point.) I worked through law school and borrowed the maximum amount allowed by the federal programs: more debt, more obligations, and still an opaque understanding of the consequences of my choices. Even as I sank into debt, I kept current on the bills that made sense to me: phone, rent, utilities. But credit cards were delightfully remote—accounts to be settled when I had the means. I still managed to secure leases for modest apartments and qualify for utilities, despite my credit score's warning to lenders.

My wake-up call about my financial straits came when I prepared to sit for the Georgia bar exam. One hurdle is the test itself, but the lesser-known obligation is the "personal fitness" application. Essentially, a candidate for attorney in Georgia must submit a detailed record of all past mistakes of substance, including felonies, misdemeanors, and credit defaults.

I pulled my credit report with a fresh eye and discovered a host of sins. Discover, Visa, and MasterCard all had vendettas against me. They didn't care about my family obligations and my noble intentions. Neither did the state bar. In order to be allowed to sit for the exam, I not only had to confront my financial failures, but I had to make amends: settle all debts and provide proof.

Doing so meant using the last of the student loans and the bulk of my law firm signing bonus to pay not only the amounts borrowed on the cards but the exorbitant interest rates that turned a $300 television purchase into a $1,000 high-interest boondoggle. I borrowed from the few close friends I had who possessed the ready cash, pleading the financial desperation that had become terrifyingly real even as I prepared to accept a post worth nearly six figures.

Forced into good behavior by the threat of losing my chance to be a highly compensated attorney, I confronted how deeply I did not understand credit and its relationship to the future I had in my head. I actually thought I was good with money. Often, I had more cash on hand than my siblings and could step in at a moment's notice to help my parents. But my understanding of personal finance barely scratched the surface. Having satisfied my immediate obligations, I learned to my dismay that my mistakes would hover like ghouls over my financial life for seven years. Seven years without the ability to qualify for a low-interest car loan and reduce the payments. Seven years unable to buy a house. Seven years with 29 percent interest-rate credit cards with limits of $500. I felt shamed by my circumstances—an obnoxious salary coupled with shabby credit.

I'd love to say that I learned my lesson after law school, and that I maintained my personal finances in pristine order. But, alas, I discovered a second way to stumble. Self-employment taxes and more personal obligations. When I left my job to run for office, I started my first company. The delight with which I received payment and immediately deposited the checks into my LLC's bank account cannot be overstated. As a tax attorney, I knew to set up my accounts for quarterly deposits into the federal Treasury. However, when Hurricane Katrina hit in 2005, my parents became the hub for their small community, providing respite and care despite the black mold growing in the parsonage and the difficulty of my mom's church to muster a full salary for her. Then, in 2006, my youngest brother and his girlfriend had a child they could not take care of due to their drug addictions. Instead, my parents took custody when Faith was two days old.

Underpaid, raising an infant, and both battling illness, my parents' bills piled up. I took on much of the financial responsibility to support them, from health insurance and medicine to daily expenses. The allure of available cash, money I should have remitted to the Internal Revenue Service, proved irresistible. I delayed my quarterly tax payments, sending cash home instead. That meant when the time came to pay my taxes, I fell behind and had to catch up—again and again.

Like any hole you dig, the trick is not only to stop digging but to climb out. Unfortunately, for those who are responsible for their own daily bread and feeding others, sometimes the ladder seems out of reach. When we become financially secure, the instinct to support everyone else can be overwhelming. Most of us are the first to make money in our family or in our social circle, but we aren't the only ones who get to spend it. The challenge here is to know how much you can afford to keep and how much can you share. Nearly twenty years later, I am still paying down student loans, and I will be for a long time unless I win the lottery or this book does exceptionally well. Perhaps you don't have the option to walk away, but at the very least, be certain you have a plan of action not to get farther behind.

The message delivered on airplanes predeparture is true: put your own mask on first before helping others. I've taught seminars for college students of color heading for graduate school, and I put them through their paces on strong applications and impressive résumés. But I also cautioned them about the dangers of financial access in college. Student loans are enticing, and they presume a certain level of both need and fiscal discipline. Only borrow what you absolutely require to survive, not to keep up with your more affluent peers. This applies equally to credit cards, which have a shorter shelf life and a higher interest rate.

Unfortunately, educational debt has no easy fix; therefore, you have to make sure you know beforehand what you are paying for. Choose schools you can afford. Investigate the academic programs before you attend and study their graduation rates and their employment statistics. I firmly believe higher education is an investment, not a debt, but that only holds true if the education yields higher returns in terms of employability and income. Certain programs are notoriously poor at delivering on either, and a degree with no value is bad debt. Also, borrow from the government before going to private lenders. Government-backed loans have lower interest rates and more flexibility, and they might be subsidized, depending on your income. Finaid.org offers several calculators to demonstrate the effects of financial options, from the real cost of loans to which jobs have the highest financial yield.

I offer similar hard-line advice for the young people who worked for me in the House caucus and for friends of every age who still find themselves fretting about their wallets. The years it takes to dig out from credit card debt (not to mention payday loans, title loans, and the like) take a toll, even when you are cash-healthy. Similarly, self-employment demands a different way of tracking your finances. Regardless of where you are in your personal or professional life, future success depends on a deep understanding of personal finances—because they don't remain private when you seek to rise. The goals, though, are consistently straightforward across the board: get out of debt, fix your finances, and plan for the future.

To get out of debt, consider the side hustle. The Internet abounds these days with ideas for ways to generate extra revenue, which should go first toward paying back those you owe. Since high school, I've found ways to make extra money, utilizing my skills in less than full-time jobs. At my performing arts high school, I learned how to operate the theater lights and eventually got gigs running the light board for shows that rented out the school's theater. In college, I got paid to do research for consultants (when research required books and library time, before the dawn of Google). Of course, my most lucrative one has been my fiction writing. With a full-time job and a second avocation in politics, I never fully maximized the potential of my writing with the publicity required to break through, but I used those advances and royalties to slowly clear away outstanding obligations. My friend Pai-Ling went in on a yoga and fitness studio, a low-level franchise without the upfront investment. Hank does telemarketing on the side, using his landline to help nonprofits ask for support. *Entrepreneur* magazine had a great list of options for the side hustle: use your home as an Airbnb, look at sales opportunities on Ebay, or run social media for a small company looking for low-cost help. If those options don't suit you, a quick Google search of "side hustle" brings up a dizzying array of options.

But this is about more than credit cards. It's all the demands on your resources. Home equity lines you can't afford or short-term solutions like title loans expose the same problem. Fixing your credit and your bank account requires structure and intentionality. For that, get support from a credit counselor or a personal financial adviser. Consumer Credit Counseling or Clearpoint.org each have a good set of options to identify and address your debt concerns. For those who think you can do it yourself (a dodgy choice), I used *Personal Finance for Dummies* by Eric Tyson. To pay down debt, the big three credit reporting agencies all offer tools that use your existing and available credit information. The reality will likely be short-term pain and sacrifice, but the long-term relief pays dividends. Address your debt issues, then guard new-found financial freedom as assiduously as my great-aunt Jeanette tended to Publishers Clearing House.

Once you've stopped digging and started climbing out of personal financial missteps, the time has come to plan for the future. Go beyond the fundamentals of budgeting and debt to understand the complexity of retirement options, self-employment responsibilities, and long-term financial support for aging parents, children with special needs, or any of the range of challenges to your personal financial health.

To maintain financial freedom, we must build wealth beyond our take-home pay or our house. That means understanding the difference between income and wealth. Over the years, my income has gone up and down, but I still have precious little in the way of wealth beyond my slowly appreciating house and bare-bones retirement account. The basic equation for wealth is savings plus assets (what you own that you can sell if you need cash) minus the debt you owe. The personal power to make choices—and to help others—increases exponentially when we expand our focus to include creating wealth.

To put the gap in stark racial terms, in America in 2013, the average wealth per household was $81,000. But averages have highs and lows. When you disaggregate the numbers, white families average $142,000 in wealth, Latinos come in at $13,700, and black families bring up the rear at $11,000. Asian Americans are closer to whites than other people of color, but they also lag behind whites. Ta-Nehisi Coates explored the historical reasons for the stark income inequality for African Americans in his seminal article for the *Atlantic*, "The Case for Reparations." The combined effects of discrimination in labor, housing, and education have compounded the struggle for wealth among communities of color.

For women, the wealth gap manifests itself first in the wages women earn. Women are more likely to be underpaid for the same work, to be in careers where salaries lag behind, and face hidden tax prejudices that siphon off their money before it can translate into wealth. The wage gap is real: in 2016, women working full-time were generally paid only 80 percent of what men received. That missing 20 percent becomes nearly 40 percent for black women and nearly 50 percent for Latinas. Losing a fifth to almost half your salary because of gender and race can hobble the most focused woman's economic plans to achieve wealth. Then America operates a tax code that has compressed income tax rates, and as a result, women who make less are treated the same as men who make more.

The takeaway: the difficulty of catching up and moving forward isn't all in your head. Systemic biases, legacy barriers, and current explosions of inequality conspire constantly to undermine wealth generation among minorities, especially women in these communities. But, as with all obstacles, our obligation is to acknowledge they exist and then fight like hell to subvert and circumvent them.

The most valuable tool in our arsenals will invariably be self-awareness and honest assessments of our mistakes and future stumbles, coupled with an understanding of the barriers in our way. To get ahead of the problem, explore your personal relationship with money and the explicit and silent claims made on your resources. Are you doing more than you should? Do you have a choice? These are not rhetorical questions—and the answers may not yield the best options. But know what you're doing with your money and why. We will make money mistakes—over and over again—but they don't have to be permanent or fatal to our dreams. Financial independence, though, can transform our capacity to take risks and soar.

FINANCIAL FLUENCY OPENS DOORS

Financial independence gives us the power to decide our futures and liberate our conception of what's possible. A similar power exists in understanding how money drives organizations— regardless of size or type. Institutional knowledge about how the corporate, public-sector, and nonprofit worlds work provides a passkey into a new dimension of influence. The more we understand, the more power we possess. Learning about the finances of a company or an organization is like learning a secret code. The ones who know how to effectively manage budgets and raise funds for projects are usually the ones calling the shots. Because we're not expected to, speaking the basic language of finances can offer a creative way to attain power in a structure not built to grant access to outsiders.

During my freshman year of college, I found myself in a battle with the financial aid office, struggling to meet costs, only to learn of a proposed tuition hike. On my way back to my dorm, I saw a flier directing members of the board of trustees to their meeting location. Since I had on my good jeans and my nice

T-shirt, I marched over to the conference room where the meeting was being held.

I knocked on the massive mahogany doors. When they opened, the secretary of the college explained in a hushed tone that the board was in a meeting. I screwed up my courage and requested to attend the meeting. Over her shoulder, I saw the president of Spelman College, Dr. Johnnetta Cole, and the board.

When Dr. Cole approached the secretary to ask why I was still standing in the doorway, I swallowed hard and asked if I could come inside. I had never attended a board meeting before, and I only vaguely understood their role. But I knew enough to know their decisions were costing me and my fellow students more money; the women who sat with me in the desultory lines outside of financial aid, praying to the Pell Grant gods for more support. We needed relief, not tuition hikes.

To her credit and my everlasting gratitude, Dr. Cole looked at me, shook her head, and then announced to the gathered cognoscenti that she wasn't aware of rules to preclude my entry. As I approached the tables where the board members sat, suddenly regretting my impulsiveness, I realized two things at once: (1) I was wearing $25 jeans that had seen many better days in a room of $1,000 suits, and (2) I had no clue what I was doing. A thin, older white gentleman, Allen McDaniel, motioned me to an empty seat beside him, and I scurried to join him. Then he slid over his board notebook, a massive compendium of the decisions of the day.

I was just in time for a discussion of the school's finances. I stared at the borrowed notebook, the lines of numbers almost dizzying. Operating revenue. Notes receivable. Nonoperating activities. The absence of zeros in the columns of numbers—then realizing the amounts totaled millions. For the next several minutes, the board grilled the chief financial officer for his explanations of line items, of missed projections and statements of account. I kept up as best I could, which is to say, not well at all. Over the next hour, the board reviewed enrollment figures, the status of donations, applications for federal and private grants, and capital improvements on the grounds. I'd never had reason to think about the interplay between the cost of tuition and the number of students who accepted admission but couldn't pay their own way, like me. Or what "development" staff did—which, it turns out, is to raise money to cover the shortfalls. Student complaints about the lack of air-conditioning in dorms, a critical issue in the humid, hot South, became a debate about increased fees for room and board.

For those of us who don't grow up at the knee of board members or business owners, the cost of things is often understood only through the personal. Trying to read a spreadsheet or a balance sheet overwhelmed me, but I was fascinated too. Lucy Vance, who sat on the other side of me, gently explained parts of the discussion, aware of how new the jargon was to me. As she whispered to me on one side, and Allen on the other, I decided then and there I would know more the next time I showed up. And I showed up again and again, earning my own board notebook and written invitations to the meetings.

My upbringing didn't prime me to analyze cash flow. Most of us aren't raised to decode EBITDA (earnings before interest, taxes, depreciation, and amortization, or just a fancy way to compare how well two companies are doing when compared to each other). When you do not come from a place of financial literacy on the personal level, confronting the corporate calculations can be paralyzing. This paralysis—a combination of fear of looking stupid and fear of actually being too stupid to understand—leads many of us to simply walk away from the math.

Still, it should come as no surprise to anyone reading this that the money matters. Which is why a leader must be conversant in the basic architecture of finance. The gentleman who handed me his board book, Allen, served as vice president at a major international financial company. Over the next four years, Allen taught me how to read financial statements and speak intelligently about fiscal issues with confidence and authority. Hovered over these statements in the quarterly meetings, I peppered him with questions about operating revenue and how nonprofits like Spelman College made money. By the end of my tenure as a bootleg trustee of the college, I had an advanced degree in understanding the books of our college. And I had the answers to tuition hikes and an insider's comprehension of securities.

Lucy, who took an interest in me as well, nominated me for a nonprofit board, which had a smaller budget but grappled with similar questions of where to get money and how to spend it. Allen's wife, Sally, started to invite me to fund-raising events, and I listened in on Dr. Cole as she raised money for Spelman College on phone calls. I eventually added economics to my studies, diving deeper into the relationships between money and policy.

Not everyone has to crash a high-level board meeting to gain the training I received. Every organization and every company that takes in money has to report it out. For-profit or nonprofit, the difference lies mainly in where the money goes, but both are extraordinary training grounds for learning. Volunteer to serve at a local organization, like the PTA or your neighborhood association. If you are ready to put your name in the hat for a larger opportunity, check out BoardnetUSA.org, VolunteerMatch.org, or Idealist.org. And when you are selected, ask to serve on the audit committee or the finance committee, whether you're well versed or not. The best way to learn is experience, and by serving in these roles, you have an insider's seat to how decisions are made. Particularly for minorities, service on these committees bolsters not only our credibility but our utility to an organization.

To gain greater competence, get to know the CFO of the entity or the head of development or someone who works in accounting. Ask for a tutorial, and be prepared to do your own homework. I also advise reading up on how to understand financial statements. Take an annex learning course at the local college on financial management. The Securities and Exchange Commission actually has a pretty good tutorial for beginners: https://www.sec.gov/reportspubs/investor-publications/investorpubsbegfinstmtguidehtm.html.

Because of my capacity gained while at Spelman and honed in grad school and law school, I usually find myself on the most powerful committees. In the legislature, which is responsible for allocating $25 billion in taxpayer dollars, I served as the only Democratic freshman appointed to the elite Ways and Means Committee. Yet, this ability has also allowed me to push back on decisions that would hurt those I am working to protect. Terrible choices are often cloaked in the seemingly impenetrable world of finance. Think about the financial collapse, which came as a surprise to most Americans, including lawmakers, in part because we lacked the ability to decipher the warning signs.

BUILDING EVERYTHING FROM NEXT TO NOTHING

Asking for money is hard, terrifying, and humiliating. We've been trained to think about money as a forbidden topic, one that only those without it discuss. Yet, we also know money is a vital ingredient to our strongest ambitions. Women have long histories of asking for help for someone else or going all in for a group but shying away from seeking support for their ideas and needs. If you believe in your vision, in the reason you're seeking support, then you owe it to yourself to ask.

Whether raising money for a start-up or asking for a campaign contribution, we must be aggressive about asking for investment. Fund-raising is essential to success. Yet women and people of color or those who do not come from money often botch the ask or refuse to make it in the first place. Deep down, we question whether we are entitled to support, or we worry that unless we can guarantee an outcome, we shouldn't ask others to take a risk. The reality, though, is that most people who make investments expect effort, not guarantees. If the potential contributor demands perfection, you can't afford the money. For everyone else, the mission, reasonably, is to establish a higher-than-average likelihood of success.

Not only do we have to get better at asking, we must also accept we can't always get financial support in the traditional ways. The admonition to raise money from your inner circle is often not a realistic option for minority leaders. Federal business loan programs, a worthy effort, often fail to reach those in struggling communities or who do not have the personal credit to guarantee their participation. And successful GoFundMe and Kickstarter campaigns are phenomena, not necessarily reliable fund-raising plans.

My first piece of advice: do not go it alone if you don't have to. I have usually started my businesses with a partner, based on the strong belief that I'd rather have 50 percent of something than 100 percent of nothing. One attribute in my partners is diversity—we need to know different types of people. This capacity to leverage distinct networks opens up opportunities to engage a broader set of investors and supporters. Do not pick a partner simply out of distinction, but scour your networks to ensure you are thinking as widely as possible about an ally in your efforts.

This applies across interests. It's the reason finance teams exist. Consider the PTA bake sale committee or the local fundraising gala. I have never seen one of these helmed and executed by a single person. The multiplier effect—that of having more opportunities due to more targets—is the core of raising money. Not only can you and your team reach more people, you also cross-fertilize awareness, which is essential to good returns.

You also need to get specific. Not only should you try to know different types of people, you and your partners must know how much money you need to raise. Understand intimately what you want the money for, and you should have a clear, well-constructed plan. Be familiar with your details inside and out. No room for "umms" or vagueness. When making an ask, you usually only get one shot unless the person with resources finds your story or product compelling. I once had to pitch a million-dollar ask standing in the meat section of the grocery store. Do not squander access by failing to prepare or relying too heavily on your ability to "wing it." The corollary is also to ask for what you need. Don't be bashful or fearful and waste your shot. Don't go into the room asking for $2,500 when you know you need $25,000. And if you need $250,000, be ready to explain why and the return on investment. There's a tendency among women and people of color—

in business and politics and beyond—to undervalue what we need because we are afraid to ask for more.

Ivy and Ben started an organic grocery store in an underserved neighborhood where the only places to buy food were fast-food chains or corner stores. They put together a strong business plan, located the perfect site, and set up their supply chain. To launch, they needed $100,000, so they identified leaders in the organic food world and set up meetings. One of their top targets owned a series of organic juice bars, and their research showed he was worth millions. In their meeting, they pitched their idea, and he seemed interested and asked for a number. Ivy, the lead on the team, asked for $25,000, and the investor agreed immediately. He told them to send over the paperwork, and they left. Once they were out of earshot, Ben asked why Ivy didn't push for the full $100,000. She flushed and responded, "I didn't want him to know how far we were from our goal." By underselling their need, Ivy caused two new problems. One, it became more difficult to raise the rest of the money they needed; and two, they delayed their ability to effectively put his money to work, lowering the likelihood he would do more. Be strategic, of course, but do not ask for the wrong amount out of fear.

Know your audience. In political fund-raising, entire companies exist to help research donors and understand who will likely invest in a candidate or a cause. Professional fund-raisers, online databases, and tech tools have converged to simplify the task of identifying potential contributors. However, to be successful, a candidate must go beyond the generic profiles to flesh out whether a particular target will be interested in offering support. Simply because a wealthy woman gave to other women does not mean she will donate to all women. Effective candidates and effective fund-raisers investigate why she gave and the issues that appeal to her.

Doing research changes everything. If you've ever seen *Shark Tank*, the show about start-ups seeking investment, you'll notice that the most successful contestants are prepared to ask for how much they need, but they also pitch their ideas to certain judges. The entrepreneurs understand who prefers athletic products and who likes ideas that can be franchised. Investors have a type of company or entrepreneur they are likely to fund. Check out their investment habits through online research and word of mouth. Determine if a particular investor prefers early-stage start-ups or late-stage companies preparing for acquisition. Join networking groups where you can share information and benefit from others' experiences. This kind of familiarity works in almost every arena. In my parents' churches, they knew who would offer a more substantial contribution to the collection plate for missionary work versus the one who would donate to a new addition to the church building. And prepare yourself for "no." A donor may decline to help, but instead of giving up, reframe your pitch, come back, and try again when the timing is better, or move on to the next prospect. But before you go, ask for feedback on what worked or how you could improve.

Jacob operated a community center in a struggling neighborhood. The kids who visited spent most of their time playing sports, but he realized that left a lot of children out, especially younger ones. He decided to add playground equipment, which proved much more expensive than his budget allowed. He did his research on prominent people who'd once lived in the community, and he surveyed his staff to see if anyone knew alumni of the community center. Together, his team identified a prominent businesswoman who had once lived around the corner. They requested a meeting and asked her to fund the playground. She refused to finance the entire project, but Jacob was ready. He then asked her to chair the fund-raising committee and host an event. She readily agreed, and by working with her to build an invitation list, Jacob discovered other potential supporters for his organization—he knew his audience, and he knew not to go it alone.

Good fund-raising also requires knowing yourself. As a first-time candidate for office, I faced two opponents in my primary race. Both had deep ties to the community, and I was a relative newcomer. I determined early on that outpacing both in fund-raising would be key to victory. I began by making a detailed, thorough, and surprising list of every person I knew who might be willing to make a contribution to my campaign. When I launched my companies, I did the same. Conduct an inventory of your personal landscape and your appetite for fund-raising. One of the most significant impediments for women running for office, particularly women of color, is the ability and willingness to raise money. We don't believe we can because we rarely see women or people of color who do. And we shy away because we do not like the sensation of asking, perhaps feeling somehow that we are seeking charity. In politics, specifically, raising campaign dollars is about asking others to invest in your vision and your values. We don't get to keep the money and public reports keep our spending transparent. In my race, I outraised my opponents $127,000 to $13,000 (combined). My capacity to fund-raise helped me move quickly in the political arena and eventually win the post of minority leader.

As a business fund-raiser, I have been less successful than my partners in raising seed capital, but I have done my share. Where I lack the wealthier networks, I excel in cobbling together lower-dollar investments. No matter what type of organization, don't rule out small-dollar contributors. We often do come from communities with limited assets, but do not assume there are no assets available. We've all read the stories of the frugal elderly woman who passes away, only to reveal a secret fortune. Or we patronize small businesses where the proprietors recall their own difficult journey to starting their companies. I strongly advise talking to these local entrepreneurs or solidly middle-class neighbors. While I wouldn't recommend a barrage of asks or a hard sales pitch, engage them to seek out counsel and advice. Allow an organic conversation to develop. Often, these conversations reveal if they possess a hidden capacity to support your endeavor. The worst-case scenario is, if they cannot provide material investment, you receive free tutelage on how to grow your project.

In the end, a money master accepts the complexity of financial decisions—personal and professional. We will screw up at some point, on some level. This doesn't always have to do with the quality of our ideas or even ourselves. Money is messy, complicated, and humiliating. Whether you are explaining why you don't have it or are trying to get it, our society frowns on certain folks having the audacity to make mistakes. We've developed fears that hold us back, that stifle our dreams or get us into deeper trouble because we refuse to ask for help and pursue what we need.

As young girls, my two sisters and I were all Girl Scouts, and we rocked at the sale of Girl Scout cookies. That's because our dad would take our cookie order sheets with him to the shipyard where he worked, and in less than a week all our slots—on three different sheets—would be completely filled. My father's sales technique, though, had something to do with it too. After all, lots of the men at his job had daughters selling cookies. According to my dad, he did so well because he asked every single person. He told us, "Never tell yourself no. Let someone else do it."

Not only must we stop telling ourselves no, we have to internalize our right to make mistakes and to use each error as an entry point to more knowledge. The more we know, the better we get and the more we can control for our destinies and the world around us.

MONEY MATTERS RESOURCES

Taking control of your finances is a fundamental skill. Check out the resources below to get started.

Personal Finances

- https://twocents.lifehacker.com/the-most-common-money-mistakes-people-make-at-every-age-1657120724 (self-explanatory)

- https://www.smartaboutmoney.org (has great tools and quizzes to understand your money habits)

- https://www.mymoneycoach.ca (excellent blog posts about specific issues like couples managing money and family obligations)

- https://grow.acorns.com (thoughtful information about how to take what you have and stretch it farther)

- *Personal Finance for Dummies* by Eric Tyson (don't be offended by the title—wonderful tutorial and easy-to-follow information)

- *The Only Investment Guide You'll Ever Need* by Andrew Tobias (not an exaggeration)

Financial Fluency

- https://www.sec.gov/reportspubs/investor-publications/investorpubsbegfinstmtguidehtm.html

- *Reading Financial Reports for Dummies* by Lita Epstein (I really like the Dummies line of books)

- http://nonprofitinformation.com/understanding-nonprofit -financial-statements (quick and easy summary of nonprofit financial information)

- *Nonprofit Kit for Dummies* by Stan Hutton and Frances N. Phillips (deeper dive, but you don't need to go to three years of law school like I did)

Fund-raising 101

- https://www.ndi.org/sites/default/files/Making%20the%20 Dough%20Rise.pdf (based on EMILY's List training, which is worth signing up for if your politics line up with the organization's politics)

- http://grantspace.org/tools/knowledge-base/Funding -Research/Training/fundraising-training (the Foundation Center offers fund-raising training for nonprofit leaders in almost every state)

- *Raising Capital: Get the Money You Need to Grow Your Business* by Andrew J. Sherman (a solid guide)

Six

PREPARE TO WIN
AND EMBRACE THE FAIL

My entire life, I've wanted to be a fabulous singer. Two of my sisters have incredible soloist voices, and my mom sings a lovely soprano when she thinks no one is listening. I attended a performing arts high school, surrounded by women and men who could belt out tunes worthy of Tonys and Grammys. However, my strongest suit did not lie in the vocal arts. My sister Jeanine once described my stylings as a guitar voice, a kind way to say I have an alto pitch that can pass muster in a smoky room filled with low chords and melancholy lyrics. Still, I harbored the dream of discovering that my voice was a diamond in the rough.

After years of fantasizing and shower singing, during my first year at Yale Law School, I decided to audition to be a singer in the Yale Law Glee Club. Tryouts were held at around six o'clock at night. I stood outside the room in a line with a collection of former scientists, anthropologists, and recent college grads who shared my aspirations to be both lawyers and vocalists. When my turn came, I walked inside, filled with nervous anticipation and a hint of pride. After all, I prepared my song and practiced it and was ready to astound with my rendition of "Give Me One Reason." But before asking for my piece, they asked me to sing scales.

Now mind you, I've never taken a single vocal lesson. I understand the rudiments of music, and I can read sheet music well enough to know the different notes, about tempo and phrasing. It turns out, though, I can't really hear the scales. A nice, talented young woman who also served as teaching assistant in my procedures class blew into a pitch pipe and asked me to sing the note. Sing it? I could barely squawk it. For an excruciating stretch of time, I discovered my remarkable inability to distinguish a G-sharp from an E-flat. I never did give them one reason.

When the audition came to a merciful end, I escaped to the outside of the graceful stone buildings that had harbored Supreme Court justices and US presidents. Humiliated, I sat on the steps, near tears, and replayed the five-minute interlude that seemed like an hour. Fellow students I would face in class the next day would now liken me to a caricatured candidate for *American Idol*. I'd crashed and burned because I couldn't sing, I excoriated myself. But that wasn't completely true.

I crashed and burned because I hadn't prepared. I had some degree of basic talent, and I thought that would be sufficient. Out of some combination of shyness and fear, I'd failed to call my sisters the singers to ask for tips. And over the years, while I harbored this goal, I never once took a singing lesson. I marched into that audition ill-prepared and I failed. Worse, I wasn't even bold enough to belt out my rendition. Instead, after fumbling through the scales fiasco, I mumbled my apologies and ran off into the night.

During my childhood, a neighbor had a little china plate hanging in the living room that read "If at first you don't succeed, try, try again. Then quit. There's no sense in making a fool of yourself." When it came to my aborted singing career, I didn't bother to try again. I skipped right ahead to the quit, a choice I continue to regret. Rather than analyze my mistakes, I gave up and buried an ambition.

What I should have done was prepare to win, power through, and, if I truly couldn't do it, embrace the failure, then figure out how to become better. A central tenet to success is to show up—again and again and again—to take an alternate approach, and keep at it until it works. And when we show up, act boldly, and practice the best ways to be wrong, we fail forward. No matter where we end up, we've grown from where we began.

LET YOUR LIGHT SHINE

In tenth grade, I went on a two-week silence strike in AP English. I refused to speak in class. I wouldn't raise my hand and wouldn't respond if called upon. I loved the class, the sophisticated reading assignments, and the critical analysis of writers' works. But I would not participate. The teacher became so frustrated, she summoned my parents to a conference. My mom and dad arrived, and the teacher testily expressed her irritation. My silent strike had drawn the attention of other kids, and I had become disruptive through my inaction. She demanded that my parents force me to participate.

Before the conference, which I wasn't allowed to attend, I explained my obstinacy to my parents. The teacher had given me a C on a paper, and she'd pulled me aside after class. She summarized her complaint with both my writing and my performance. "You use too many big words, Stacey." I asked if I had used the words incorrectly or out of context. She told me that wasn't the problem. Instead, it was that she didn't feel I should use that kind of language when other kids weren't able to do so. Plus, she found my choice of independent reading material too advanced and dark. With a generous smile, she encouraged me to curtail my efforts to outshine others in class.

I took her at her word. I stopped speaking. My parents recounted the story to her, asking if I had misrepresented the situation. The teacher conceded I had not. Then my mom made the same inquiry I had. Was I using words inappropriately or sloppily? The teacher said no, but my broader vocabulary made the other students feel less accomplished. As my mother recalled the incident, she and my father set her straight about holding their daughter back. "We send her to school to learn how to think, not to be told what to think." Thirty years later, my dad recalled, "She wanted you to be quiet so she would feel better."

Inherent in the idea of "the other" is a disturbing expectation—we should not be prominent or noticeable. The current political discussion of "identity politics" begs the question of whether these differences of race, gender, faith, or more should be given prominence beside the traditional expectations of what pundits consider the norm in political discourse. Business is not immune to the phenomenon of hushing difference. With numbing regularity, annual studies chime out about how few women lead companies, and we can name practically every CEO with melanin. Announcements about minor progress—hiring the first woman to lead GM or a person of color taking the helm at a Fortune 500—come with great fanfare. The clever jujitsu of these discussions is how we then celebrate the unicorns, forgetting for a moment that it's the twenty-first century and long past time for firsts and seconds.

Winning begins with an admission that we deserve to be seen and heard as essential members of a community. Instead, what we confront is a tacit call for meekness, to hide our lights lest we become too noticeable and change the discussion. In practical terms, the translations are clear: don't stand out, don't speak when not spoken to, and accept the rules and the way of things. This is the commentary we hear from the instant we dare to make demands on a system not designed for our arrival. Show *meekness*—such a mealy, insubstantial word with such grave consequences.

Jocelyn worked for a law firm as an administrative assistant. Over the years, as she typed up important documents, she'd developed a knack for spotting issues others had missed. The partner for whom she worked appreciated her efforts, often praising her diligence. One day, she knocked on the partner's door. The senior attorney invited her in, and Jocelyn shyly held out her graduation certificate. She'd quietly taken paralegal courses, and she asked the attorney to be a reference when she applied for an open slot on the paralegal team. To her surprise, the attorney balked. She warned Jocelyn that the post of paralegal might be too hard for her and urged her not to apply. While the attorney appreciated her skills, she reminded Jocelyn that she'd been a secretary for a long time and would be safer staying put. Rather than go to another partner or speak with other paralegals on the team, Jocelyn quietly tucked her certificate in her desk and remained an assistant for several more years.

The habit of not going beyond others' expectations can transmute self-awareness, until the meek begin to believe they are less than. Out of experience or fear, the habit becomes permanent, and its practitioners never move forward, never stray too far from the familiar. Cautionary language takes on the ring of wisdom: "Stay in your lane." "Don't rock the boat." "Wait your turn." "The world's not ready."

The reality is quite different, however. When we practice boldness, the antithesis of meekness, the world adapts. Each minority community's advancement that we've seen over the past decades, be it people of color, women, or the LGBTQ+ community, has displaced the previously held norms, which had seemed insurmountable before. However, to get there, we must cease being participants in our own oppression. The real success of the call for meekness is when minorities come to believe the message as much as those in power. Harriet Tubman once declared, "I freed a whole lot of slaves. I could have freed a whole lot more, if they'd only known that they were slaves."

Jocelyn had a spark, but she allowed another's disbelief to quash her ambition. Meekness, then, is not entirely the fault of those in power. For too many, the tendency to fall in line comes easily and becomes internalized. We have all sat in meetings and refused to speak up. Why? Probably because we didn't know everything about the topic. Now, remember that meeting. Did a man, younger in age or in experience, raise his hand and say exactly what you were thinking? Did the boss applaud his ingenuity? Or, more important, if his idea wasn't on point, did anyone boo or hiss or ignore every other idea he ever had?

Sam Park, a former intern of mine, decided to run for the state legislature against a two-term Republican incumbent and committee chair. We sat in my office, and I listened as he explained his rationale for running. His mother had been gravely ill and, without the Affordable Care Act, would likely have died from her disease. The GOP representative he wanted to replace had opposed Georgia's expansion of health care to the working poor in our state. I pointed out to Sam that he faced three immediate obstacles: he was a Democrat in a Republican district, a Korean American in a predominantly white community, and openly gay in a deeply religious area that still grappled with the issue of sexual orientation. But his bold plan and enthusiasm captured my imagination. That day, we made a deal. If he proved his willingness to do the groundwork it took to win, and kept me apprised of his progress, the House Democrats would invest in his race.

He built a diverse campaign team, studied the district, and began to canvass the area, knocking on doors. Like clockwork, I received regular reports of his progress, and our team kept tabs on his data. I asked our polling firm to test his new standing in the district, and the numbers were astonishing. Sam had closed a massive deficit against a better-funded opponent. We joined the effort, and Sam unseated a GOP incumbent on election night, becoming the first openly gay man elected to the state legislature and the first Korean American Democrat. Sam's preparation to win, his refusal to wait his turn, and his boldness in asking for and working for our help are pitch-perfect examples of how to prepare to win.

To find boldness requires active discomfort: doing that which forces you beyond your bright lines. For some, to be bold is to walk into a meeting and take the reins. For those who are less confrontational, it is to walk into the same meeting and, rather than taking the reins, insert their voice for the first time. In any context, boldness can start small. It can mean seeking out other views from those who have also grown meek or deferential. Or looking for collaborative ways to shine during a project. Perhaps it is as simple as praising the ingenious but flawed comment of a colleague and helping guide a discussion about how the idea could be better. Maybe it looks like running for something. Or volunteering to lead a committee when you've only been a member. We can redefine each boldness to reflect our uniqueness and our strengths, draw the line and then push it farther and farther away.

Sometimes, bold action is about your willingness to change who you are and what you think you want for your life. In 2003, I faced a stark turning point in my career. At the time, I was a well-paid tax attorney at my law firm. Sutherland Asbill & Brennan had been exceptionally generous with me, allowing pro bono time to be spent in service for newly elected mayor Shirley Franklin, the first woman and the first African American woman to lead the city of Atlanta. After her election, I chaired a commission for the mayor and, in my capacity as attorney and as chair, I gave testimony on legislation proposed by the commission. On one of the days of testifying, I was assailed by city council members opposed to the legislation. After a particularly grueling session, I stood outside the city council chambers, licking my wounds. City attorney Linda DiSantis walked up and introduced herself to me and asked, "Well, how's it going?"

I looked at her—and this is after I've been excoriated by the council—and answered in all honesty, "This is so much fun!" Indeed, after three years as a tax attorney, to stand before a group of women and men committed to the public service and to press my case for a change in policy was exhilarating, if difficult.

Surprised by my response, she gave me a quizzical look, then she nodded and left. A few days later, I received a call asking me to meet her for breakfast to talk about the city's law department. I drove to the breakfast, planning to politely decline any job offer she might make because I had no interest in leaving my lucrative and flexible job at Sutherland to become a staff attorney for the city of Atlanta law department.

I met her at a little diner, and over eggs, she shared with me her vision for the law department. Only a year into her job, she'd spent her tenure fomenting change in an entrenched bureaucracy, which was quite a change from her previous job as a vice president for UPS. Linda acknowledged the reputation challenges but insisted that the office was filled with smart lawyers ready to deliver. She wanted to change the way legal services were provided for the purposes of policy making. To achieve her goal, she needed a division of the law department to bridge the gap between law and policy.

After a thoughtful discussion about the contours of the division, she asked if I wanted to be a part of it. I replied hesitantly, "It's an intriguing idea," but I knew I wouldn't leave a private-sector job to join as a staff attorney. Then Linda explained that I would head up this new division.

Timidity warned me that at only twenty-eight, I had never run anything as large as the division she described. Meekness urged me to demur, as I had no municipal legal experience. And logic demanded I not give up my private-sector salary for a city job. But boldness, the willingness to take risks, and the drive to do the hard work of learning this role demanded I say yes. So I did.

One caution, though. Crossing bright lines, being bold, has consequences. Not everyone will embrace the more aggressive you. The backlash might be subtle, like no longer being invited to participate in events or meetings. Or it could be starker, like a blocked promotion or a termination, or losing an election.

As I run for governor, I have found a whole group of potential supporters turned off by actions they see not as bold but as contrarian. In 2011, the state of Georgia faced the collapse of a signature program, the HOPE Scholarship. Nearly twenty years before, Democrats had crafted a program to guarantee pre-K, technical college, and college education for any Georgia high school graduate with a B average. For years, the program succeeded, but during the Great Recession, and due to a variety of factors, funding was running out.

I became the minority leader just in time to confront this horrible situation. Republicans had taken sweeping control of the legislature, and we had a new Republican governor who could reasonably claim a mandate for action. The Republican solution to the crisis called for cutting pre-K, restricting the grant for technical college, and imposing a standardized test requirement on the college scholarship. Within our Democratic caucus, debate abounded. Some wanted to solve the problem, while others wanted to force the GOP to take responsibility for their actions. My role, as both political leader and legislative leader, meant I had to weigh both goals.

When faced with the choice of doing nothing or working with Governor Nathan Deal to negotiate a better solution, I chose to negotiate. I understood that simply protesting the GOP proposal guaranteed its passage: House Republicans outnumbered Democrats 112 to 68, and they needed only 91 votes. Faced with certain harm to our constituents, I secured a two-tiered program, where kids who didn't do well on standardized tests still received most of the old scholarship. I also asked for and got a $20 million 1 percent low-interest loan program to make up the difference. Technical college students kept more funding than originally offered, and I preserved the full pre-K program. Democrats joined me in voting for the final bill, yet hard feelings about taking any action lingered. By working with Republicans, I angered a number of Democrats. I understood, but I disagreed.

So it's true: if you are bold, you will alienate others. There's no way around it. The best approach is to plan what you are going to do. Not only plan your action and anticipate the reaction, but then think through what you are going to do with what you've done. For me, I consistently have to consider the impact on my family, on my future plans, and on my ability to be successful. Boldness lies not simply in having the thought but in claiming ownership, accepting responsibility for moving it forward, and then dealing with the consequences. Prepare to win, but also prepare to fail, always using boldness as your guide.

FAILING AND FLYING

No matter how much preparation we do, sometimes we're going to fail, and our task is to embrace the failure. Risk taking inevitably leads to missteps or bad decisions. Unfortunately, admitting mistakes is a fundamental skill too few of us learn. In part, this is because we have been taught it's wrong to be wrong. As children, making mistakes serves as a training ground for adulthood. We learn where not to stick our fingers, how to study for tests, and the right way to parallel park. However, we also begin to crave the positive reinforcement of success and avoid the flush of embarrassment when we mess up. Over time, like laboratory mice, our instinct toward pleasure overrides our desire to learn by picking the wrong option. Worse yet, the pursuit of success becomes justification for bad behavior, a necessary step toward power.

Failing forward, that is, taking risks and potentially falling short, has a utility. Invention, discovery, and empires are built of chances taken with high degrees of failure. But losing or screwing up serves as a form of mental cartography, which results in a map of what we should avoid and a preview of the terrain for better outcomes. One of my business ventures, Nourish, produced bottled water for babies and toddlers to make feeding easier. Just add formula, shake, serve, and go. We sold our products in hospitals, airports, and hotels—anywhere parents and infants might need last-minute help. Our dream was to break into grocery stores, like Whole Foods and Kroger. We'd gotten a test at a Whole Foods in Arizona, and they liked the product enough to place a large order. Unfortunately, at the time, all of our products were hand-assembled. To meet such a substantial order, we'd have to automate, which cost more money than we had. We went to banks, to alternative lenders, to personal contacts, but no one wanted to loan us the money. We hung on for a while, but until we could automate, we were forced to stay small and unprofitable. Facing the reality, we wound down operations: a business failure.

That was until one of the lenders we'd met with asked for our consulting help. John Hayes had started other financial services companies, but he thought he had a way to solve problems for companies like Nourish—where we had a customer but no way to deliver the product without money. Our consulting team worked with John to research and then build on his idea, examining the financial technology industry and how we could bring our different skills together to solve this problem in a unique way. Together with John and two other partners, Lara and I cofounded NOW Corp., a financial technology company, and this venture has been a great success, moving millions of dollars to small businesses like Nourish, helping them accept orders and grow. A failure became a map to success.

With any bold decision, our personal fears wrestle with our ambitions, arguing about whether the risk is worth the reward. For those who seek true leadership and wish to leverage real power, we also have to use failure to fly—to *fail forward*, as the saying goes. The ability to have this conversation with yourself, honestly and unguardedly, sits at the center of achievement. My boss in the city law department once told me about experience: some people have thirty great years but others have the same crappy year thirty times. They sit still, holding fast to mediocrity and inertia, and claim not losing their post as a victory. But leadership demands boldness, which necessitates failure because each action taken, each decision made, will carry a consequence. If you have been bold, and if you have been ambitious, then you will have risked reputation and credibility.

In the aftermath, if your gamble failed, the temptation to fudge the results or omit the truth will rise exponentially. I spent much of my first year as a tax attorney in private practice cramming in knowledge and trying to learn on the job without committing malpractice. Among my cases was one of the top nonprofits in the country. The organization faced an audit from the IRS and several questions about tax decisions that they'd made. I volunteered to take on a critical line of research, eager to show my usefulness.

I spent hours poring over documents and studying decisions, reading through laws and codes. During one of my nights of inquiry, I read through a set of regulations and found a line in the tax law that seemed to be the silver bullet. Convinced it solved our problems, I quickly wrote a memo and sent an e-mail to the partner and to the senior associate proclaiming my discovery.

Jim, the partner, scheduled a conference call with the client and the IRS, and my memo was a key element in the discussion. I arrived at work the day of the call, a bit early just in case more prep work needed to be done. In my office, I decided to read the lines of code one last time. As I read through, my stomach dropped. On this, my fourth or fifth reading, I noticed a line I had skipped. A line, that when read together in its totality, said the exact opposite of what I thought it said. More important, the code completely bolstered the IRS's opinion and their stance, placing our client in terrible financial jeopardy.

At that point, we had thirty minutes before the call. I cowered in my office, knowing that to tell the partner of my mistake would be a stunning blow and could end my career. Perhaps, I thought, they won't use what I've told them. Maybe, I rationalized, the IRS will buy our explanation. But in my head, I could hear my parents and all the women and men who helped support me and who had taught me better. What I could hear in the silence of that office was the canon of a life ethically lived: you made a mistake, own up to it. And don't you dare let somebody else take the fall.

So I rose from my desk and walked down the hallway to the partner's office. He answered my knock, a bit impatient. I haltingly explained my mistake and waited for the explosion. He watched me for endless moments, with a look of disappointment and confusion and grave irritation with my existence on this earth. Then he said, "Fine, go on back to your office."

I left his office, returned to my own, sat down, and started packing because I was certain that I had just ruined a major client's case and would soon be seeking other employment. After nearly an hour in conference with the IRS and the client, Jim came to my office. I braced myself for dismissal and prayed silently that I wouldn't beg. All he said was he was glad I told him and handed me a new case file. Then he walked out of my office and I started to cry. Tears of embarrassment that I had made this mistake. Tears of relief that I still had a job. Tears of sincere gratitude that I had been taught to tell the truth.

If I had kept it to myself, I might have gotten away with my error. But I could just as easily have found myself out of a job when a better lawyer discovered my mistake. As minorities, we are held to higher standards—both in our actions and our reactions—especially when we seek to do the right thing. Nevertheless, we are best served when we accept the credit due when a project goes right and take responsibility if it's wrong. If we've done the best job we can do and we adequately prepared, and if we've made the right decisions and the result is defeat, then we accept the consequences there too.

THE BEST WAY TO BE WRONG

If you are going to make any decisions, take any leadership actions at all, live a fulfilling life, then you are going to be wrong. The goal then is the ability to admit that you have done so and use that information to move forward. Knowing how to be wrong is fundamentally about honing the ability to admit that you don't know. Effective leaders are able to say to the person they want to impress the most: "I don't know." As minorities, we feel an intense pressure to be right, and some of us, myself included, find great comfort in defining our value based on what or who we know. Thus, I work hard to remind myself that the point of daily life, of learning and taking action, is to gain more knowledge. If you already know everything, you might as well stay home. Wise leaders know how to be wrong, and they take even more comfort in the fact that they cannot know everything.

We've all been in situations where someone looks to us for answers, and we are tempted to say what we think—not what we know. Social media abounds with guesses masquerading as knowledge. I remember watching former Atlanta mayor Shirley Franklin in a meeting with CEOs and others who could help or break her agenda for the city. She got peppered with questions, and deftly responded, until one stymied her. Instead of offering a half-answer, she smiled and said, "I don't know, but I'll find out and get back to you." As one of her attorneys, I was tasked with finding out the answer. I don't quite recall the issue, but I will never forget the confidence with which she admitted an area of ignorance. Since then, I have learned lots of ways to say, "I don't know." My favorites are, "I have some ideas, but let me do a bit more digging" and "Here's what I think, but I could be wrong. I'll check." Or I direct the person to the proper authority and I make the introduction myself. The best way to admit you don't know is to always couple it with a way to find out.

We must be willing to learn; however, gaining that knowledge can be a humbling experience. A minority leader who can be wrong has had the audacity to approach rivals or co-workers or subordinates and say, "Teach me." But let's be honest. We have to be careful who we ask for help or to whom we admit ignorance. Here's where your version of mentors—that personal board of advisers—can be helpful. Remember to reach out to those who may have safe ways to help you gain access or tutelage. Have your resources ready, as I did with Laurette while learning to be a better manager. I began setting aside time every week to sit with her and discuss challenges. I took notes of my concerns and brought them with me, to get her advice. I did the same during my meetings with the city attorney. In the legislature, I identified colleagues who demonstrated a skill or an expertise I admired. Some I asked to join me for lunch to discuss their approach. With others, I requested an open door to come and visit. On tougher issues, I've reached out to more experienced or prominent people, seeking a quick call. These requests invariably make me queasy because I'm nervous about their reaction to my outreach. Occasionally, a high-profile person has refused to speak with me, and several times I was simply ignored, but at least I made the effort.

Being wrong also extends to our judgment of others. It is a searing hurt to learn that you're dead wrong about the values of another person, a revelation that can leave you feeling betrayed and angry and stupid. That's often why leaders refuse to admit they are wrong. Not only have we at times chosen the wrong person, but sometimes we have been wrong in gathering opinions, in weighing our own feelings, in seeing the truth of another's character. Whether the choice was a personal one or a professional one, we must be able to admit that we were wrong about others.

Belinda, a former political reporter, decided to move into political lobbying. Because Belinda was both a woman and a person of color, she had few colleagues to whom she could direct questions. She reached out to a handful of more seasoned veterans in the industry to seek their guidance, including David, an older lobbyist of color. He cautioned her to wait before approaching certain politicians, under the theory that she shouldn't contact them in their home districts when they were away from the capitol. Belinda delayed her outreach, as advised. In January, she began to make her rounds, only to find that the legislators had already committed to David's clients on their positions. What she realized was that most of the deals cut for the legislative session occurred in the representatives' districts months before work began. The lesson cost her clients, but it also taught her who to trust.

Over the years, in every facet of our lives, if we are willing to risk, we will lose. And we'd all like to think that the scale would show we've been right more times than wrong. We create change when we eschew the instinct to only play when we know the outcomes. Instead, we are more creative and more courageous when we push ourselves beyond the complacency of clear victories. Nearly every leader can regale you with mistakes made and transformative failures. However, the best leaders understand how they stumbled or hesitated in their response, and did the right thing anyway. The most significant successes come from letting your light shine, embracing failure, and getting good at being wrong.

TRYING AGAIN

Making the Most of Mistakes. List three times you have taken risks in your personal life, work life, or community life. What were the consequences? How did you feel immediately afterward? How do you feel now? Would you do it again?

1.
2.
3.

Know That You Don't Know (and Admit It). Note times you have been tempted to pretend you know the answer.

- Why did you feel that you should?

- How did you handle the question? What happens when you say you do not know?

- What happens if you pretend you do know?

Ignorance Is Bliss but Knowledge Is Better. Pick an area you wish you understood more about in your job, in your organization, or in your personal life.

- Who can you ask to explain the subject to you?

- How does it feel to ask for help? What have you learned about yourself by learning this subject?

Accept Being Wrong and Give Credit for Being Right. Identify an experience when someone took the credit for the work you did. Now, identify a time when you blamed someone else for a failure.

- How could you live that moment differently?

- Pay attention this week to opportunities to give credit and take responsibility. If you approach these opportunities consciously, will you act differently?

Seven

MAKING WHAT YOU HAVE WORK

Rebecca, a patient advocate at a local clinic, had been asked to lead a team applying for a funding opportunity on behalf of the organization, but she didn't want to do it. The award would give $100,000 for the service project and $25,000 to the project leader. Larger organizations were also competing, led by seasoned professionals with higher profiles than hers. They had gleaming offices and fund-raisers on staff. Rebecca had never written a grant application, and she initially balked at applying, unable to believe she could compete. Then she read the application more closely. Winners would be selected based on the content of the application, past accolades, and "community endorsements" or testimonials.

The clinic lacked the internal resources of its counterparts and was little known outside its small section of the city, but Rebecca had built strong personal relationships with her clients over the years. She agreed to spearhead the project and began to reach out to former and current patients, asking for their help. In a matter of weeks, she'd amassed more than a thousand responses, more than the other applicants combined. When the clinic won the prize, Rebecca sheepishly recounted her initial hesitation. She had never completed a fund-raising proposal or won an award, but she knew how to do her job and how to help people. Those skills, more than professional wordsmithing, bolstered her credibility and secured the prize.

One of the best things about being in the minority is the fact that limited resources often lead to extensive creativity. We become very clever at exploiting whatever is available, growing our arsenal from the scraps left around, and becoming a sort of MacGyver of power building. During my third year in the Georgia legislature, the Republican majority planned to ram through a mass of dangerous legislation on "Crossover Day." To streamline the process for creating new laws, the legislature, years before, required a bill to pass either the House or the Senate by this political D-day to stay alive for the rest of the legislative session. Thus, for the last ten days, the House only voted on Senate bills and the Senate only voted on House bills—a compulsory kumbaya.

While Crossover Day solved a turf war between the House and the Senate, it didn't help the minority party much. The GOP had deftly closed all the loopholes they'd used to undermine Democrats when they were in charge, which left Democrats out of power and out of options, or so it seemed. Not yet in the leadership of our party but used to being outnumbered, I had an idea about how to disrupt the GOP's plans. Working with my friend, Representative Brian Thomas, we convened a tiny group of fellow rebels to plot, code-named Strike Team. Crossover Day began at ten a.m. and had to conclude by midnight, which gave us the weapon of time.

With only fourteen hours available, and dozens of bills to consider, every second counted. I'd carefully read the rules of the House, which allowed each legislator up to twenty minutes' worth of questions about every bill. But no one ever tried to use all their time. Well, if seventy-five Democrats, with twenty minutes on *each* bill, all ask questions, the day would slow to a crawl.

Once Crossover Day began, we moved into action. One by one, bills were presented by their authors. Members of the rebellion began to push their buttons to request permission to speak. Again and again, routine measures faced interrogations that delayed their passage, sometimes by five or ten minutes. Unaware of our shenanigans, the Republicans scrambled to figure out why previously mute members of the legislature now had intricate questions about blueberry farmers or coastal tides. For hours, we tangled up the works.

I was standing near the Speaker's podium when I heard him ask his chief lieutenant, "What the devil is going on here? Why is everyone asking questions today? Do you think the Democrats did this?" His lieutenant scoffed, "Of course not, they aren't this organized." In the end, we forced such long delays that some controversial bills had to be dropped. More, though, our fellow minority party members saw the people in power yield to their inquiries and flail as we stymied their efforts. They weren't quite sure what happened, but they delighted in the results.

At the core of leadership is the issue of power—the ability to secure what you need and the capacity to influence others to help you get it. So, the questions for those in search of power abound: Who has it? How do we get and wield it? What do we do when we have less than the other guy? What do we do when we lose it? While the self-help and business books are rife with discussions of leadership, the bald conversation of gaining power—especially for those who rarely hold it—is unusual. As a result, too often, we in the minority miss opportunities because we don't know what we're looking at or looking for. Minority leaders do not have the luxury of traditional power, which comes with experience, access, and information. But when we understand how power works and how we can fight back and gain some for ourselves, we can rewrite the rules.

First, when a minority leader has few weapons in her artillery (little money, limited access to power, a weaker public narrative, etc.), exploiting the situation is itself a potent weapon of the minority. We cannot fight a war with resources we don't possess—so we must inventory what we do have and figure out how to use them in unexpected ways. Those assets might include access to information, a familiarity with the situation others don't possess, or the ability to withhold participation from a process. The goal is to examine everything and leave nothing out.

In addition to using situations to our advantage, leaders need to understand the difference between position and power. A lowly post that has access to important decisions can allow us to find moments to show our own command. During a campaign I managed, Ashley Robinson served as a field operative, one of many tasked with knocking on doors and then inputting the data into our computer systems. One evening, Ashley showed me a set of patterns she'd noticed about the voters we were contacting. This was a pattern only she saw because her job was to type up the notes, and her insights helped me redeploy our teams. I was so impressed with her initiative and thoughtfulness, I brought her on to later projects, from spearheading a voter engagement project to assisting a statewide candidate for office. Her consistent performance—taking advantage of roles to expand and deepen her experience—led me to hire her as my chief of staff when I became the minority leader. Ashley went on to lead the BLUE Institute, which has trained dozens of people of color to become campaign leaders, and she has founded her own successful political consultant shop.

The converse is also true—having a fancy title does not confer the full authority to act. The allure of titles, financial acquisition, and the veneer of respect can cloud the reality of where we really stand. We've all seen so-called leaders in our organizations who cannot effectively accomplish their roles, but continue to coast along on title alone. Knowing how to honestly assess where we are can help us map a path to more effective leadership and decision making.

Access to real power also acknowledges that sometimes we have to collaborate rather than compete. We have to work with our least favorite colleague or with folks whose ideologies differ greatly from our own. Not only does this require doing something we may not like, it can also alienate those who share our distaste and see cooperation as a betrayal. But working together for a common end, if not for the same reason, means that more can be accomplished. Often, these are small wins, but they add up.

At their core, though, authentic leaders know what we believe and why, in order to have a clear sense of our direction. Without that internal compass, we get lost in the pursuit of power, forgetting our purpose and compromising our integrity. But putting it all together, we can make real change.

TAKING POWER MEANS TAKING STOCK AND TAKING TIME

In stories about fighting and winning, the most exciting ones have a simple narrative: the little guy faces the behemoth and, through daring and cunning, triumphs. Or a poor family strikes it rich and saves the day. Then there's the reversal, where what looks like defeat becomes victory. However, for every straight victory, minority leaders must be prepared for the slow-burn tales too, where victory doesn't arrive quickly, the resources don't look like gold, and losing becomes the crux of the story.

Sometimes, winning takes longer than we hope. When time is not on our side, we have to settle in and prepare for the long haul. That requires setting expectations early for those who follow you, and adjusting to the challenges of a long fight. In 1964, Fannie Lou Hamer defied President Lyndon B. Johnson and threatened his election, going on national television to excoriate the Democratic Party's insensitivity to the plight of blacks seeking a vote in the South. Johnson countered by holding a rival press conference, forcing national cameras to focus on the White House rather than on the Democratic National Convention where Hamer held court. The Mississippi Freedom Democratic Party lost its bid to be seated in 1964, but the delegation gained full recognition in 1968, a delayed victory but a win nonetheless.

Texas state senator Wendy Davis held the floor of the state Senate in 2014 for eleven hours to block a regulation to roll back reproductive choice. She beat the bill that night, but the GOP passed it in the following session, leading a newspaper to declare that she'd won the battle but lost the war. The temporary win and later loss seemed to agree with the headline, but one of the aspects of holding power is understanding the long game—that battles add up over time and create space for others to feel embold-

ened to act. And sometimes, a single act of defiance raises awareness and action, which in Davis's case meant the federal court
decision that later blocked parts of the bill from taking effect.

Other times, wielding power demands we use the resources at
hand, which can seem so common as to be worthless. We can
become conditioned to believe we must have the same assets, or
worse, that whatever we have at hand is inherently inferior. But
the creative ability of minority leaders lies in excavating the valuable in what is available. My business partner, Lara, told me
once about the apocryphal origins of bottled water as a hot com-
modity in the beverage aisle. Coca-Cola, the purveyor of the
eponymous soft drink, produced Coke by mixing its secret syrup
with tap water it then carbonated. This meant the company possessed millions of gallons of water in bottles, waiting for an infusion of liquid wealth. But a smart employee realized that the
water itself had value if properly packaged and sold. Thus, Dasani
(and then Aquafina and others) was born, and millions of dollars
have been generated from a simple decision to use what was
already at hand. I mean, think of it, paying money for a container
of what flows for a nominal sum from our house pipes.

As a young girl living in a community with precious little ability to demand what we desired, I spent hours reading about
those who'd been able to bend destiny to their will. One of my
favorite novels was *Silas Marner*, a story about a wronged man
haunted by secrets who nevertheless finds happiness. I enjoyed
the story, but I found myself wondering about the author. The
brief blurb on the jacket told me little about George Eliot. Other
novels, *Middlemarch*, *Adam Bede*, and *The Mill on the Floss*, were
referenced for readers who wanted to read more by the writer.

Instead, I decided to read more about the author, George Eliot. Turned out, Eliot had secrets too—George had been christened Mary Ann Evans. Born in Britain in the 1800s, she refused to be relegated to a certain type of writing or thinking. Instead, she realized if she published under a male pseudonym, she could write the stories she wanted and, as a result, her works received wide acclaim. Eliot leveraged her education and cleverness to circumvent the restrictions placed on women writers of the time.

When I founded the Strike Team, I had only been in the legislature a short time. I doubted anyone would have listened to my ideas for disrupting the legislative process. Instead, I turned to a trusted colleague who had more seniority and I shared my ideas with him. Representative Brian Thomas, in turn, agreed to convene the initial group of legislators under his own banner. Like George Eliot, I used a foil, which increased rather than diminished my efforts. Now—hear me clearly—I am not suggesting women sublimate their ideas and their power to men, nor should any person of color subjugate themselves to move forward. I do recommend that you identify the source of the obstacle to making your voice heard and find a way to use it to your advantage. Once the Strike Team convened, Representative Thomas turned over the meeting to me and, as we discussed, he consistently reinforced my ownership of the idea—after everyone agreed to participate. Similarly, Eliot gained her own reputation as a woman of letters, revealing herself as the author of the celebrated works *after* publication, much to the chagrin of men in the industry and after achieving higher sales for herself.

As much as resources matter, so does the ability to lose well, and learn from it, as part of the trek to power. Lara once introduced me to her friend Sara Blakely, who turned a pair of reworked pantyhose into a $20 billion industry and, less than a decade later, became the world's youngest self-made female billionaire. I met Sara at the start of my business career, and she described how she was getting ready for a party but didn't care for the silhouette created by her white pants. As she happily recounts, she took a pair of scissors to a pair of pantyhose and Spanx was born. But in that same conversation, Sara recalled her attempts to sell her idea to massive department stores who discounted her idea—clearly disbelieving a young woman could have come up with a solution to a problem they hadn't thought about. Her persistence, using a combination of grit and charm, brought Sara to the attention of industry leaders and, eventually, to Oprah herself.

Though losing or failing may seem like a setback, these stumbles are inevitably a part of the process to power, particularly for anyone using nontraditional means to get there. I learned this the hard way. During the 2010 legislative session, the Republicans broke their own procedures to pass a surprise tax bill I feared would hurt the families I came to the capitol to represent. More than $200 million was stripped away from education and human services to fund wealthy senior retirements and jack up fees on working families. Righteously indignant, I hurried over to the Democratic leadership and shared my objections. Determined to stop the debacle, I went to see the Speaker himself to plead my case, but to no avail. The Speaker heard my concerns but determined the amendments could proceed. Unable to stop the bill through the logic of my arguments, I pulled out the red legislative rule book, thumbing through for a little-used provision I had vaguely recalled. I would use it to make my concerns known to the entire body.

As I stood at my desk, heart racing and microphone in hand, the Speaker reluctantly recognized me, and I announced my intention to challenge the ruling of the chair. That is to say, I challenged the authority of the Speaker himself. One of the last people to do so had reputedly lost his committee chairmanship and his office. But I did it anyway, and besides, I had a crappy office and no real perks in my current position. In the moment, when I announced my motion, I heard gasps throughout the chamber. Which should have prepared me for what followed. The Speaker's face tightened in fury, but he had no choice but to call for a vote to rebuke his determination.

He needn't have worried. Despite knowing I was correct, and sharing my opposition to the bill, only thirty-nine of my one hundred and eighty colleagues were willing to speak up, out of fear of reprisal. My bid failed miserably, and the offending bill passed easily. One of the dangers of guerrilla tactics and challenging power is the reality that those who stand to benefit may not stand with you.

Indeed, I soon found myself temporarily out of favor with the Speaker, with whom I had previously had a decent relationship. Someone jokingly moved my parking space decal to a shadowed corner of the parking deck, a no-man's-land far from the other legislators. Colleagues on my side of the aisle muttered about how I'd invited the wrath of the Speaker down upon them all. However, I also drew the attention of other members, ones who had dismissed my quiet and solitude as weakness. More of them began to pay attention, and when I launched my bid to become the next minority leader, I had more supporters than I'd imagined. They may not have been willing to fight with me at the time, but they admired my courage and ingenuity.

For most of us, we will always begin several steps behind, out-matched according to the traditional standards. Maybe you have less formal education than a co-worker who wants the same promotion you do. Or perhaps your community regularly gets ignored by its elected officials. Our mission, then, is to figure out how to navigate around the standard expectations and to influence the outcomes by setting our own goals. Try making a list of accomplishments and experiences that can substitute for a degree—and asking your boss what else you can do to demonstrate you're ready. To get political attention, try organizing your neighbors to visit your elected officials in their offices and set up a community scorecard to keep track of how responsive they are. The trick is understanding what we have available to work with to achieve our best ends. But we need to realize that when we take the risk, the reward may be a while in coming.

POSITION ISN'T THE SAME AS POWER

When Lara and I founded our first venture together, Insomnia Consulting, we melded our two sets of expertise—hers in commercial real estate and business, mine in government infrastructure and law. Lara served as CEO because she would be the forward-facing leader of the company, and I served as COO, leading our internal development, managing our resources, and keeping us on track. In our subsequent companies, a manufacturing company and a financial services firm, I again took lesser billing.

From the beginning of my foray into business, friends have questioned why I didn't insist on co-billing. After all, I did half the work in our first two companies. As one friend asked, "Why give up so much power to her?" What I told them is what I firmly believe: what you are called is not the equivalent of the influence you hold. Despite our collective human fascination with status and the naming of things, real and discernible differences exist between title and authority.

Titles convey the set of responsibilities a person holds, and they stand as clear markers of intended influence. Particularly in hierarchies, we use titles as guides to the quickest means to finding answers. Even in these pages, I rely on the position I held as minority leader to convey my expertise and garner respect for my insights. Names matter; labels matter. We should always pursue the highest title available and fight for the labels that reflect our clout.

However, to rewrite the rules of power, never allow the position to limit your sphere of influence and control. When Lara and I initially discussed our titles—how we would present ourselves to the business world—I fretted over the labels, but not because I disagreed with how we had assigned our roles. I absolutely did not want to be the one recruiting clients, plus I had other responsibilities as a legislator. Nevertheless, I wondered if I would be undervalued because she was the CEO. Having not come from the corporate world, I felt my angst grow. On the legal papers I'd drawn up, we were partners. Equals. That wouldn't be the reception we got in meetings, though. Later, when we sat in rooms pitching our products, my fears proved true. Clients sometimes dismissed my ideas or deferred to her on final decisions.

More frequently, though, I found ways to insert my expertise into the process. In one of our ventures, I convinced a client to take us on because I understood public finance and offered him intelligence on his past failed endeavors with cities and counties. In other meetings, I demonstrated my prowess as an innovative thinker while also validating my partner's role. Over time, I learned when to assert myself and when to hang back, learning not to be fazed by who got more attention or credit.

The other job of understanding the distinction between position and power is knowing which one you actually want. My ego balked at not having the highest title in our companies, until I realized I actually didn't want the role of CEO. Sage Works, the consulting firm I started when I left the city of Atlanta, had exactly one major client. To build the kind of business Lara and I envisioned, we required a leader who knew how to solicit those jobs. I had never done the type of business development we required, and she had. Plus, I also had my responsibilities first as a new legislator and then as minority leader. I also wrote novels on the side, which meant my sole focus would never be our company. Leadership can be alluring, but you should not accept a position unless you can effectively meet the obligations that come along with it. I wasn't willing to be the woman in complete charge, which was okay. I just had to admit the truth and find my place of power.

Also, a well-titled position can create a false sense of leadership— just because someone has the office, do not assume he can do the work. As team lead in a printing firm, Patrick managed ten colleagues. He relegated the bulk of his work to them, then used their output to charm his superiors in upper management. Kareem, the director who worked for his team, typically took on the role of training the staff, helping with projects, and aligning assignments with workload. When a malfunction threatened their primary product, Patrick was summoned to an emergency meeting, ill-prepared to explain what had occurred. As they demanded answers, he was forced to bring Kareem into the meetings to help deconstruct what failed. Team members rallied around Kareem's leadership and resolved the malfunction, illuminating who had effectively been in charge. When a promotion for VP opened up, Patrick threw his name in for consideration. The management team, though, realized Kareem had been doing the job for a while and offered him the post instead.

No one likes to be taken for granted or taken advantage of, but both happen in organizations—corporate, public, or nonprofit. The opportunity for command may come in the form of overwork, sloughed onto your plate by a lazier boss. Or when tasks come along that no one wants to tackle, the means to become a micro-boss shouldn't be ignored. I see these as chances to build skills, gain experience, and position oneself for the next big opening.

While I worked at the law firm, I took on several pro bono assignments, much to the chagrin of the executive leadership. Their irritation morphed into modest appreciation when my efforts introduced the firm to new clients and gained attention for our community engagement. As deputy city attorney, I volunteered for initiatives and, over my tenure, expanded my portfolio to include paralegal manager and the de facto acting city attorney when my boss was away, despite being the newest person in the leadership team. At the capitol, in my second year, the Democratic leader tapped me to be the chair of the newly created fund-raising committee for our caucus. I reported to the caucus treasurer but did 100 percent of the work. In that role, I met

donors and lobbyists who normally would have ignored a legislator in her freshman term. Instead, I expanded my base of support and was better positioned to run for minority leader when
the time came.

Another critical lesson in position versus power is not simply
doing what you're hired to do; the ones who move up also do what
needs to be done, even if it's not their job and no one asks them
to do it. Nourish, one of my companies with Lara, manufactured
bottled water for babies and toddlers. We launched the business
with just enough start-up capital to pay for equipment, produc-
tion, and a limited marketing budget. Unable to pay ourselves or
others, we brought on a young intern during her senior year of
college. Our focus had to be on finding customers for our product, which took most of our time. We asked Brittany to take on
the simple task of updating our website and logging invoices.

Using her initiative, she took the job of cleaning up the site as
an opportunity to teach herself how to build webpages. She then
found potential marketing partners by offering to co-brand our
products, using our invoices as a guide to who might be interested in working with the company. By the end of her internship,
she'd established our marketing division and created a full-time
job for herself. She leveraged her position to establish her bona
fides and became an invaluable member of our team.

CHANGE THE RULES OF ENGAGEMENT

Power is directly tied to winning, and for those of us on the
outside, the definition of winning must be adaptable to the

circumstances. This can sound like a cop-out, but I'm dead serious. Those who hold power have no interest in handing it over. They like it. Those of us who want it may not want or need all of it—or sometimes not all at once. Instead, I rely on two approaches: first, I distinguish my idea of a win from that of the ones in power, and second, I locate who can help me achieve my objectives, often through an activity known as power mapping. The concept of power mapping began in social justice circles with the goal of identifying who had control or influence, understanding their relationships to others, and then targeting them to promote social change. I have developed my own approach to a personal power map, where I lay out the problems I want to fix, pinpointing who can help, who can influence, and how I can get the work done.

Resetting the objective comes first because you need to know your mission, which may be unlike what those around you expect. I love television and one of my favorite shows is *Star Trek: The Next Generation*. A main character, the android Data, yearns to be human, but his greatest utility lies in his extraordinary robotic capacity—he's faster, smarter, and stronger than anyone else aboard the *Enterprise*. He processes information at extraordinary speeds, is never distracted by emotion, and can punch through metal walls.

In the episode "Peak Performance," Data plays a game called Strategema against a humanoid strategist, Kolrami. The assembled crew watches, excited to see the famed master of the game fall prey to the intellectually invincible Data. So they are all in disbelief when Kolrami soundly defeats Data. Stunned by his loss to a mere person, Data runs diagnostics on himself, trying to assess how his programming let him down. He plays Kolrami a second time, losing yet again. His friends rally around him, urging him to put the defeat in context. But, like the humans he longs to emulate, Data replays the game on an infinite loop in his head, unable to find his flaw.

He removes himself from duty, leading to a confrontation with his boss, Captain Picard. Picard reminds Data that it's possible to lose without making any mistakes and, even if mistakes are made, they are not a sign of weakness. A chastened Data returns to duty and challenges Kolrami to a third game. The scene cuts to Data battling Kolrami, with the once-triumphant Kolrami flicking his fingers furiously as Data calmly engages the game. While I've never been clear about how Strategema is played, this final scene has become one of my parables for minority leadership. As the score grows higher and higher, Kolrami abruptly quits, forfeiting the game to Data, who is declared the victor.

When asked about my political philosophy as a Democrat in the Deep South, as the leader of outnumbered legislators, as a black woman often operating against better-positioned opponents, I recount this story, because it encapsulates so much of the minority experience with competition and the pursuit of power. Data is different from his peers, yet his differences can be seen as both asset and liability. He plays the game and nevertheless finds himself losing. When his friends ask Data how he beat Kolrami, he explains that he realized that outright defeat of a master would be impossible.

Instead, Data reframed his objective—not to win outright but to stay alive, passing up opportunities for immediate victory in favor of a strategy of survival. He changed the rules of success and, by doing so, reframed how his achievements should be judged. For Data, the goal was to outlast his opponent, not defeat him, which is sometimes the best outcome. My lesson is simpler: change the rules of engagement.

Wherever I am, regardless of the type of role I'm in, I try to begin by understanding what I want to accomplish. My goals are usually based on what's possible in the short term and where I can get to over time. The next step is to figure out the obstacles to my goal. From my experience, the barriers fall into a few consistent categories: a person, a tradition, a system, or just old habits. Here's where tweaking the rules really comes into play.

If we want to create change on most issues—income inequality, the company's sales protocol, or simply getting the neighborhood association to pick a new security firm—power mapping is essential. The tough questions and the most daunting issues need champions in government, innovative entrepreneurs, and courageous nonprofit leaders to build effective systems and infrastructure for now, in order to lay the groundwork for progress that will last long after.

Power mapping sounds tedious and overly complicated, but it's neither. It may also sound calculating and harsh, and that's a valid critique. At its core, a power map identifies who is in charge of what and forces you to think about how you interact with each person. The practice helps you clarify your goals and recognize potential obstacles. Once she became a minister, my mom had a mantra for the objective of her church and its parishioners: to meet people where they are, not where we want them to be. For her, this translated into an outreach ministry to send members into the community to understand their needs. I heard in the saying a power-mapping tool, and I've borrowed it ever since.

Once I understand who is involved, I determine if they are willing to help me or if they'll be challenges to navigate. Now I am the daughter of not one but two ministers. When your parents are in the business of saving souls, you learn at a fundamental level that winning isn't everything. Smart leaders internalize the limits of their own actions and search for counterparts who can help them move farther along. In business, I do this by developing partners—I have had a business partner in almost every company, someone to balance out my skill set. In politics, I sought out the advice of other legislators and advocates, seeking guidance and honest critiques of my leadership. My voter registration effort, a massive undertaking, began with my calling one of the brightest women I knew and asking her to write a proposal so we'd be able to do it right from the start.

Collaboration and compromise are necessary tools in gaining and holding power. In my job as the leader of the Democrats, I was supposed to fight with the Speaker of the House, a Republican, but some of my fondest and most effective moments are the ones that begin when we call each other "my friend." We don't say this cynically but in recognition of a longer history that will survive after the battle of the moment.

Given the scope of the issues we face, too often we wrongly map out power by assuming the right leader is the one with the most brilliant mind, with the most unique approach, who can go it alone. Moreover, as minorities, we think that to be valued, we must take all the credit and be the author of every solution. I assure you, this thinking is wrong. The best ideas and the best policies are typically collaborative, and those that succeed are the product of a community.

When a woman, a person of color, or a millennial prepares to lead, she can be lulled into believing that the winner will be the resident genius, and the only way the work gets done is alone. Worse, we talk ourselves out of power because we haven't *already* solved the problems. The reality is much simpler: the ones who deny themselves a place in the room where the work gets done will be the victims, not the leaders. Too often, race, gender, and age convince us to sacrifice our potential power because no one has told us we have it—or that we already have access to enough of it if we read our power map.

BELIEF AS AN ANCHOR FOR SMART POWER

The final essential element to changing the rules of engagement is to know what you believe and why you believe it. Sounds basic, but leaders often find themselves adrift because they never bothered to understand who they are and what they think is true and real. Beyond the easy labels of party or philosophy are the deeply held convictions that shape those labels. This isn't simply a political problem, though politics provides the easiest example. We have to pick labels to run, even in nonpartisan races; our messaging signals where we stand. The sleuthing is harder in the private and nonprofit sectors, and the convictions are subtler. Ideology informs how leaders think about hiring and firing, about pay raises and work assignments. And we all have some form of ideological framework. No position or industry exempts us from having to know our own minds.

Beliefs are not inherently problematic; indeed, they are critical anchors. If a leader doesn't have any hard-core internal holdings, she runs the risk of opportunism—making choices because others do so or because it's easy, not because the decision is correct. The anchors of belief should never weigh down the capacity for thoughtful engagement and reasonable compromise. Effective leaders must be truth seekers, and that requires a willingness to understand truths other than our own.

In political circles and, more quietly, in boardrooms or meetings, the idea of "flip-flopping" has become a death sentence to power. When a person admits that new information has changed her perspective, we are quick to recoil as though every pronouncement or decision should be absolute and immutable. I reject the idea that beliefs cannot evolve with better information. Smart voters and smart colleagues understand that new information leads to new ideas or understandings and possibly new beliefs. The trick is admitting you know more than you used to and that smarter is better. Most people can accept that a person can change what he or she believes, as long as that change is authentic and grounded in a true examination of philosophy and reality.

Knowing what you believe holds great power because you will be called upon to balance the needs and desires and the arguments of many. A leader represents not only those who share her core values but those who despise all that she holds dear. Politics, for example, is a constant test of my capacity for learning. I know legislators who have a definite, firm, and unshakable opinion on everything before any new information is shared.

Talking to them is exhausting.

This is because public policy—usually—isn't good or evil, or even that interesting. It is mundane and routine, and it cuts across neighborhoods, nations, and ideologies. So when a belief allows only for a single myopic focus, a solitary filter that has no room for debate, leaders miss the true role of government and of public policy. The same goes in the office where doing what has always been done is the reason to keep doing it wrong, or where fear of the unknown paralyzes decision making. These short-sighted leaders are easy to spot. They are the ones who have a definite opinion about every headline and who give you the answer before you ask the question. And if you can't point out who in your circle of colleagues is that person, it just might be you.

I do have core beliefs, but I don't have an unshakable position on every issue. I accept that I may not know enough about a situation to render immediate judgment, which is why I attend meetings and read everything I can. Whether you are a politician or an executive or an active citizen trying to improve your community, always keep clear in your mind the difference between policy and belief. Policy is what you should do. Belief is why you do it. But when you believe too much, you often are willing to do too little.

In creating a path to power, our responsibility is to inventory what we have at hand: rules we can manipulate, discounted or overlooked resources we can repurpose, or job opportunities we can enhance. I understand the fear of doing so, a deep sense of personal underestimation that says if you thought of it, so did someone else. Maybe so, but there's no harm in trying it too. Acquiring power creates an opportunity to redefine what it means to win. My success tends to happen when I take on challenges that others refuse because the risk is too high and because it's hard to see the reward. Winning from a position of strength is not a hard task, but leading from a position of weakness is risky. However, when a person can take advantage of that weakness and transform it, the return on the risk can be extraordinary.

POWER MAPPING

In personal power maps (unlike the social change versions), the issues are directly related to your goals. However, the process is generally the same.

1. **Identify your problem or goal:** What are you trying to accomplish? Be as specific as possible but clear and to the point. Example: I would like to change careers from banking to running an animal shelter.

2. **Identify the key decision makers related to that goal—by title or position:** Who can help you? Who can stop you? Who should be part of the process?

   - Help: The head of the local animal shelter; the volunteer coordinator I work with every week at the shelter; my friend who works with the city's animal control unit.

   - Stop: The head of the local animal shelter; my boss, who would like me to stay in my position; my spouse, who is worried about the loss of income; other financial obligations.

   - Part of the process: My spouse; my kids; my friend Taylor who wants to work with me eventually.

3. **Map the relationships:** If you have a relationship with the person, identify how close you are and if you can directly contact him or her.

a. If you do not have a relationship, think about who in your circle may know the person.

b. If you don't know anyone or don't have a connection, determine if you can find contact information.

4. **Reach out to targets:** Make contact with your targets. Discuss your problem and solicit advice or concerns. Carefully note what you learn. If you need to, engage others in your relationship map to ask on your behalf.

5. **Make your plan:** Collect your feedback and revise your names from step 1. Determine if you can sway anyone opposed or if you actually require the support. Then set out your action steps for how to move forward and what your asks will be.

Eight

WORK-LIFE JENGA

I reject the idea of work-life balance. It's worse than a myth. The phrase is a bald-faced lie, designed to hang over the human psyche like the Sword of Damocles. Balance presumes an even distribution of weight, of value. Anyone who has ever held a job or taken care of another person or lived understands that no set of tips or tricks can create a lifestyle equilibrium. The relentless pursuit of this unachievable end results in hours of self-loathing, tons of unused apps on our phones, and diminished quality in the time we actually spend in pursuit of either.

Instead, I believe in Work-Life Jenga. You know, the game where you stack up these seemingly equal-size blocks to form a perfect tower and then proceed to pull them out one by one, restacking as you go along. The goal of the game is to make as many moves as possible without destroying the tower, even as it sways and lists, trying to accommodate the reordered blocks. So too, in Work-Life Jenga, the expectation is not one of balance;

it's one of strategy and making the best of each move, one block at a time.

In early 2006, my parents lived in my mother's parsonage, the home provided to her as the pastor of H. A. Brown Memorial United Methodist Church. An aluminum gray FEMA trailer squatted in the old carport, a metal respite from the black mold that had taken up root in my parents' bedroom. The parsonage, like the church across the driveway, had been hammered by Hurricane Katrina less than a year before. Mom and Dad still waited for insurance company payouts and the necessary reconstruction of both home and church. They were also waiting on the birth of their second grandchild, courtesy of my brother Walter. Walter and his girlfriend had met during a recent stint in rehab, where both received treatment for drug addiction. Their sobriety wobbled, but they fell in love. Struggling to stay clean, Raquel moved into the FEMA trailer as her due date grew closer.

By the day their child Faith was born, both Walter and Raquel had relapsed and were using again. As a result, the state removed newborn Faith from their custody. That afternoon, Mom and Dad welcomed their first granddaughter; five days later, my parents became her guardians and, a few years later, her adoptive parents. At fifty-seven, they'd been gifted with a new life to raise, while grappling with the terrible addiction that plagued my brilliant youngest brother. Meanwhile, H. A. Brown, the church my mom built, where my father led the outreach ministry, continued to serve as a hub for hurricane relief for families whose recoveries hadn't occurred as quickly as FEMA and other agencies had hoped.

I watch in awe as my parents, undaunted and now nearing seventy, raise my niece and welcomed my grandmother into their home. Dad travels to Atlanta several times a year to be treated for recurrent prostate cancer and attendant illnesses, with my mom faithfully by his side. Facing her own health challenges, Mom tries to fit in exercise between Faith's violin recitals and reviewing her homework, never doing as much as she'd like. Their perseverance doesn't surprise me, though. Their priorities, determined by family and storm and community and faith, morphed beyond their planning but not their capacity.

I've heard friends of my family marvel at my parents' stamina and question their own ability to manage difficulties. They measure themselves against my parents and find their own efforts wanting. I reject the false equivalence because what I learned from my parents' commitments and choices is to do my best.

In the same year Faith was born, my business partner, Lara, had recently given birth to her son, Connor, and I had just been elected to the state legislature. That autumn, my friend Lisa Borders called me with the crazy idea to bring a Women's National Basketball Association team to Atlanta. I grew up watching sports, with a healthy appreciation for athleticism, a working knowledge of the different games and scoring, and absolutely no interest in participation. But it's hard to say no to friends.

Lisa, Lara, and I met for lunch in September, and Lisa explained her vision. The three of us would convene a group of women and perhaps some trusted men to do a version of *Field of Dreams* for the WNBA: build it and they will come. In her mind, this crew of movers and shakers would recruit investors and an owner for a new basketball franchise in our hometown. Lisa, an avid basketball fan, held two key positions—an executive with one of the city's largest development companies and the role of Atlanta City Council president. Lara had the business experience and access to investors. I brought legal expertise and a talent for organizing projects. We sketched out a list of potential partners, our Circle of Trust, who would help us identify and grow our team of dreamers. Over the next year, we indeed found investors and a team owner, and we brought the Atlanta Dream WNBA franchise to Georgia.

None of us gave up our primary occupations, and none of us went to work full-time for the WNBA team. (Lisa did eventually become the president of the WNBA.) During the same year, Lisa maintained her responsibility for her aging parents; Lara and her husband, Casey, raised their son; and I helped my parents with the aftermath of Hurricane Katrina, Faith's arrival, and my brother's slide back into addiction. We found ways, somehow, in our separate lives, to rearrange the pieces and keep moving.

At any given moment, we each face a barrage of obligations, often disparate and distinct from what we thought would happen when we woke up. From the tragic to the common to the extraordinary, life refuses to be divvied up into careful slices of time. No technology can manage to overcome the realities of reality. Everyone has a story to tell about what she intended to accomplish and how life intervened.

The drive to achieve, regardless of the goal, will inevitably lead to a false internal narrative about how successful we are, especially when compared to an idealized notion of what is possible. What Work-Life Jenga allows for is the truth: we are going watch in horror as the block we removed forces the tower to waver or we might just knock the whole structure over with a wrong move. *So we cheat.* We prop up the tower and stuff blocks back into place and try to find a better move. Or we rebuild and start all over again.

FIRST THINGS FIRST

First things first might be a cliché, but it's a useful one that means prioritizing what matters most to you and believing there is no wrong answer. When it comes to figuring this out for yourself, the careful binary of work or life entirely misses the point. We may have jobs we go to or families at home, but either can be hard work. I spend most of my time engaged in politics and social justice, but this is my life. Letting go of the finite distinctions and the moral judgments we hear beneath our choices clears the way to allow us to set priorities without condemnation.

I look at my siblings and marvel at their distinct ways of crafting their priorities. My youngest sister, Jeanine, is a dynamo. A PhD in evolutionary biology, she has a thriving career, two adorable boys, and a loving and thoughtful husband. I admire the attention she gives to her sons and the playful relationship she shares with her spouse, where even after nearly a decade of marriage, they have a standing date night and go see horror movies. Jeanine tries to fit exercise into her daily routine, although she bemoans the trainer she goes to see to keep her fitness goals on track.

From behind the locked bars of his cell, our brother Walter fights for his sobriety and to prepare for release. We send him new books regularly, his agile mind eager for new ideas. He calls home to speak with his daughter, eager to maintain a relationship strained by his mistakes—both criminal and personal. When he and I connect, we debate politics and talk about his future plans.

Richard, the older of my two younger brothers, is an extraordinary father and an attentive husband. To watch his three kids' faces light up when they see him is a moment of transferred joy. He loves his wife and has a fulfilling career helping troubled children in need. He's also our brother Walter's best friend, the one most likely to take the late-night call from him when he struggles.

Appointed as a federal judge for life, my sister Leslie sits on the bench and serves her newly adopted community. Her closest friends live farther away, but it is a testament to their deep bonds that they trek down to Southwest Georgia to visit her, sometimes from as far away as California.

Andrea, our eldest sister, is a college professor who has taken on several young mentees through the Posse Foundation program, which pairs first-generation college students with teachers and administrators. One Thanksgiving, Andrea brought my sister Leslie and me up to Kentucky to help cook the holiday meal for those who couldn't make it home. She chairs committees, writes books, and heads a national anthropological organization.

For me, I turn back to my carefully tended spreadsheet of life, started in college when heartbreak and righteous indignation fueled me. Most of the items are pretty well on track, except for an incomplete column for personal relationships. The items are straightforward: meet the man of my dreams, fall in love, and have two kids by the age of twenty-eight. When I missed the initial deadline, I shifted it to thirty-two, then forty-one. Now, I keep the column on the sheet, but the deadline is blank. I have no idea if I will marry or have children. One is a question of fate, the other biology.

As the author of romance novels, I have been asked on more than one occasion about my love life. As I got ready to run for governor, we did focus groups, and one of the topics was how harshly I would be judged for my single status. The kindest question about why I'm not married is usually prefaced by acknowledging how busy I am. Less thoughtful ones accuse me of being too ambitious and of prioritizing my professional goals over my personal life. Older women, of every racial category, warn me that my college and graduate degrees are a turnoff. Men who speculate without invitation cite my tendency toward strong opinions. And occasionally, I do worry they are right, that I should have made better, more balanced choices. Of course, I reject the notion that I've gone over the proverbial hill, but the evidence that all these detractors might be correct meets me at home alone every night.

Then I remind myself why I don't meet their standards for successful womanhood: wife, mother, CEO. Because the standards are stupid and arbitrary and make very little sense in universal application. Without realizing I'd done so, years ago, I decided to ignore how society told me I should behave because what I was doing turned out pretty well. I set a direction for my life, and I have tried mightily to stick to my path. I have erred along the way in romantic relationships (a book for another day) but not because I picked work over life. Instead, I have consistently probed my core to determine what holds my interest and where I want to spend my time.

One of my choices occurred during my third year of law school, when I completed my first novel. I'd been thinking about writing for years, had written poetry, dabbled in playwriting and screenplays, even songwriting (my specialties were country music and Christian pop). The last year of law school is notoriously rigorous. Yale Law School, my alma mater, had a reputation for churning out presidents (Clinton and almost Clinton), Supreme Court justices (Sotomayor, Thomas, Alito), and high-profile attorneys. With unsurprising regularity, classmates announced clerkships and job offers, boasted softly about salaries and perks. As a soon-to-be Yale attorney, I had checked the boxes on a few items: job offer, check; journal article, check; novelist, not yet. Since the modern-day legal fairy tale of John Grisham, nearly every budding attorney has a novel waiting for the airport book-stands. I was no different. Approaching the final months before adulthood took complete and total hold of my life, I decided my priority would be writing one too. The original story, one of espi-onage and intrigue, became a romantic suspense novel. I sent off the pages to an editor, and she bought the manuscript. Soon, I had a book deal, and more pages to write.

Like any good story, mine came with a twist. My book deal earned me car note payments, but I wasn't about to buy a car with my avocation. Writing, however, had always been about more than money. I love the craft, the care of developing a story, plot-ting out the movements of my characters, delving into their lives like an omniscient voyeur. Writing fueled me, and my task was to make it fit into my life. I went to work every morning, practiced my trade as an attorney, and on weekends and holidays I typed away. I assumed a nom de plume, Selena Montgomery, to separate my fiction from more academic publications on tax policy. Eight novels later, I put Selena aside to focus on the task of leading the House Democrats. I miss her and the stories she has yet to tell. I have other novels in various stages of completion, including a teenage amnesiac superhero story, a kids' book about the mishaps of a nine-year-old alien, a finished legal thriller awaiting edits, and a final Selena Montgomery story to wrap up a trilogy I published years ago. Writing has been both outlet and avocation, activating a part of me that now lies dormant. I struggle with the absence, and I long for the days when I can again turn my attention back to fiction and penning the stories teeming in my brain. However, as is bound to happen, my priorities have shifted, and I have to believe I will return to my love one day soon, just not now. Putting first things first—be it a relationship, a job, or a newly discovered passion—will be a consistent test of addition, which requires a readjustment, sometimes a subtraction.

Our priorities should ideally engage heart and head. I am grateful I rarely have held a post where I had to choose one over the other. Whether it's a personal relationship or a professional activity, the goal is to care about what you do and have it stimulate your mind. Since balance is a myth, we have to decide for ourselves which way the scales tip. I tend toward head more than heart, which means I have to nudge myself into exploring why and what I may be missing by doing so. I don't spend as much time on my social life, a valid choice, but only if I do so voluntarily. When I find myself setting priorities based on fear or judgment, I reexamine my decisions. Priorities change, and our most authentic behavior lets us adapt to the new needs, walking away from what was, even if we once gave it top billing. First things first allows for the introduction of new information and the necessity of better options. By prioritizing our interests, whatever they may be, we can distinguish between what we want and what we're told we should desire. And in the process, we find out what matters.

First things first also requires us to prioritize our time. President Dwight Eisenhower is credited with inventing a system I've found useful in managing time and people. He distinguished between important and urgent and looked for the interplay of the two. Urgency speaks to how time-sensitive an issue may be. Importance categorizes how much of an impact the action can have. The most critical priorities should be both urgent and important—time-sensitive and change-making. In terms of Work-Life Jenga, these are the choices where you could not have foreseen the timing but the results matter, or where procrastination has led to delays of critical projects until the last possible minute. You've got urgent and important, important but not urgent, urgent but not important, and none of the above. With apologies to President Eisenhower, I go with *Gotta Do*, *Need to Do*, *Oughta Do*, and *Might Get Around To*.

Under Gotta Do, the test is both if it has to happen now and if it matters if it happens. Rebecca has a paper due in the one graduate studies course that's a prerequisite for her thesis. The day before it's due, her girlfriend falls ill, and she spends the next several hours waiting with her at the hospital. Her choices are both important and urgent, and picking which one takes first spot is the crux of Work-Life Jenga. We face smaller, less stark moments of urgent and important that come at us all the time. In personal relationships, we don't want to forsake a loved one's needs for our own, especially if the other option can seem selfish. Invariably, we'll make the wrong call. Sometimes, the only block you can choose is the one right in front of you.

Next is Need to Do. Whether it's family, friends, projects, or personal time, give yourself permission to invest early in the items that need to happen because they impact your ability to keep your options open. Like a savings account, we can build up a reserve of goodwill and accomplishments, something we can dip into when the unforeseen happens. Lindsey had worked for me for several years, and she consistently demonstrated dependability, a strong initiative for new ideas, and a great attitude. When a crisis happened, she needed time off and had no idea when she'd be back. I had no hesitation granting her the unlimited leave because I trusted her. To me, having her engaged as a whole, healthy person meant giving her time off—and she'd shown me she understood what was important time and time again.

Oughta Do tends to happen when someone else's important needs require your urgency. Usually, in these situations the urgency is the result of another person's sense of first things first. My tenure as a manager and as an older sister honed my intuition about the burning matter that's been set on fire by someone else's lack of action. You might be managing your church's choir or a team of midlevel execs, and the rubric remains the same. The question to ask is whether their crisis will prevent you from achieving your goals—your firsts. In every organization and nearly every family, someone dominates in the urgent but not important category. Their strident demands or sheepish apologies have the same effect, that of diverting you from your objectives to answer the moment of their needs. By appraising your own priorities, you can assess whether meeting an urgent request is necessary or can be delegated. And whenever possible, do delegate. Untold amounts of lost time have been ceded to the urgent but not important, but you don't have to play.

Might Get Around To is exactly what it sounds like. The least relevant demands on our time are the ones that are not important and not urgent. These requests do not advance your interests, and there's no reason to deal with them now. Of course, this list often includes the things you want but don't need. The point of prioritization is not to completely ignore these—they may be fun—but to be certain they don't take up space that should be used for what you really do need. So leave those blocks untouched and move on, knowing you can always come back.

By giving ourselves permission to put first things first—without judgment or false comparisons to others' choices—we create space for finding time for what matters and making the most of our lives.

DON'T DEAL WITH JERKS

When Lara and I founded our firm Insomnia, we had five rules, my favorite of which was "We don't deal with jerks," though written with a bit more colorful language. (For the curious, the five rules were [1] Life comes first, [2] Don't deal with jerks, [3] Only take projects that engage our head and our heart, [4] If it can't change the world, we don't do it, and [5] Sleep is optional.) In the business context, we agreed to fire any clients whose values failed to align with our own or whose boorish behavior made our work harder than required. The "jerks" label extends to flaky friends, the colleague with the constant emergencies, and the guy who always borrows but never lends. I've expanded the description to cover a host of people who are essentially unkind, those who place their needs above others and have little patience for the issues that don't involve them.

Only twice did we have to invoke our "no jerks" rider, by mutual agreement. One person misled us, more than once, and though we'd had a prior friendship, we both realized he wasn't an ethical business partner. The other one simply had a terrible attitude, constantly complaining without providing concrete actions we could take to improve our engagement. After a while, we realized he reveled in never being satisfied, and though he paid on time, we dreaded getting summoned to meet with him. So we fired both of them.

Terminating the relationships meant losses of lucrative contracts, both at times when money for the firm had become tight. Leaving clients put us in jeopardy, but the relief when we were done with them more than compensated for the financial loss. Developing an effective work-life strategy demands sacrifices, and successful players recognize that there will be real, tangible costs and are willing to absorb the hit. Being willing to walk away from that which does not serve us allows us to move in the direction of a better opportunity.

Although we styled our firm as "infrastructure consulting," we took on a range of clients that tested our rules and exactly how little sleep we could get away with and still do good work. In a single year, I wrote a case study for the NASA Lunar Module, studied the intricacies of desalination of ocean water, and crafted a plan to convert a capped landfill into a mixed-use development. Our diverse clientele appreciated the broad range of skills we possessed, and Lara and I welcomed the intellectual rigor of solving their problems. Without putting our mission into more complex terms, "We don't deal with jerks" spoke to the obligation of dropping any activities that drained the limited time and resources we had.

We've all taken on projects or accepted responsibilities we didn't want or weren't prepared to handle. More commonly, the martyrdom happens because we think no one else will do it, and we convince ourselves someone must do the dreaded task and that someone is us. Sometimes that's true, but more often than not, the problem is that we actually don't like to say no. But saying yes doesn't make you a better person, and it can quickly become a reason to whine. Work-Life Jenga forces us to carefully examine our willingness to forfeit our mental health under the guise of doing good. We aren't doing anyone any good when anxiety replaces satisfaction and our well-being.

In extreme cases, "We don't deal with jerks" means looking in the mirror. When we've delayed happiness, allowed our energy to be sapped away, and compromised our values, the results eventually manifest themselves. I spend a great deal of my time delegating responsibilities or handing out assignments. Every so often, I reach out to the lowest-paid members of our teams to ask them about interactions with me. Am I short-tempered, distant, or terse? Do my actions reflect the values I espouse in our work? I do the same with my siblings from time to time, as a check against becoming the jerk in the relationship.

Whenever we reach for more, we begin to juggle what we're already carrying. The tension mounts, and we all lash out, in our own ways, from time to time; it's an inevitability. The most effective leaders figure out their triggers, and they empower those around them to sound the alarm. This part is particularly salient for women and people of color because we are held to higher standards of behavior in most spaces, even among our own communities. Besides, being nice and suppressing our feelings can be taxing in its own way. We become numb to our own emotions, oblivious when they leak out, and start to damage relationships or even our health. Because we are typically unlike the majority of people around us, our faults are often magnified, and our responses to crises get measured against a perfect standard of behavior. Therefore, our "jerk" barometer has to be hypersensitive and also self-directed. So get in dialogue with those closest to you about how you are

acting and reacting. By welcoming the critique and respond-
ing well, we improve our ability to do well in every other aspect
of the game.

THINK BIG AND ACT SMART

We all want to hedge against disappointment, be it in our personal or professional lives. I've never met an effective leader
who sets a direction and then simply walks away, hoping to
arrive safely at the goal. Good leaders are always at the ready
but not always at the front. The strategy here is to hoard the
time you have for your pursuits by being as miserly about how
you spend it across the board.

After I published my novels and began to grow a broader
reputation in the civic community, news of my dual identities
spread. Time and again, I heard a variation on the same question:
do you sleep? Those who asked often laughed as they did so, making light of the serious inquiry, because embedded in the ask
was a self-directed criticism: why can't I do it all? I do sleep, though
less than the recommended amount. But I reject the idea that success requires sleep deprivation. My approach, I explain, is not
trying to do everything at once. I prefer to think big and act
smart.

I get a lot of things done because I do what I'm good at and
let others shine in their roles. In my senior year of college, I served
as the Student Government Association president, an important
role for student life. If you ask my dearest friends from Spelman,
and I have, they will tell you I was well known but not very popular. I rarely went to parties, never attended homecoming, and
spent more weekends inside than out on the town, which is why

I quickly turned over responsibility for student social activities to hand-picked advisers and gave them free rein within a budget. At these events, which I had to attend as a matter of courtesy, I roundly praised their efforts and gave them complete credit.

On boards, at work, I intentionally identify the strengths of others and encourage them to excel. Their prowess allows me to focus on the areas of my greatest capacities. I am a strong writer, I know a great deal about policy on a range of fronts, and I am an accomplished speaker. However, others with similar abilities may never be seen or heard if I am constantly the one doing the work. By not trying to be everything to everyone, I don't waste time or energy. I may try to learn from them, but I try never to *become* them. Usually. I admit to being a bit of a tyrant when it comes to jobs where writing is critical, but even there, I'm getting better. I hope.

In my current campaign, I have a capable manager who has skills that far surpass my own in field operations, and who has actually run statewide races before. However, having run campaigns before, I am tempted to interfere more than I should. Thinking big also means knowing your goals and using the best resources to get there. I work hard not to ask Lauren too many granular questions, and I make a concerted effort to stay away from most staff meetings. Becoming governor is my heart's desire, all the more reason to trust Lauren and her team to help me by staying out of the way.

That said, I am not abdicating my position as the candidate, nor will I hide my expertise in certain areas. Instead, I share my concerns with Lauren, empowering her to offer solutions before I interfere. But if I am our best resource, she'll invite me to the conversation, secure in the knowledge that I understand when to leave.

Doing a job another person can do, particularly better, is a waste of a precious resource. So, before you jump in with both feet, check if you are absolutely necessary to get the work done. Regardless of the task or which category it falls into, the analysis is the same. Are you an essential element for success? If so, go all in. If not, go away.

To think big and act smart, we also have to tend to our connections. Family, friends, and co-workers all have a role to play in maximizing the time we have and the quality of our interactions. Work-Life Jenga is a multiplayer game, where our actions intersect with someone else's stack all the time. The tendency to become myopic about our own ambitions and our challenges affects everyone. Winning, then, means checking in on our teammates and really hearing the answers.

Eliza Leighton and I had been close friends for nearly twenty years when we decided to launch a social media app together, The Family Room. We began the project with great excitement, although she worked full-time as an executive director for an organization while I had the legislature, NOW Corp., and writing projects going on. From the start, she took on the hard task of fund-raising and leading the development of the product, and I focused on the back-office stuff, like creating our materials, our website, and our financials. At a certain point, Eliza stepped fully into the role of CEO, while I continued to do my bit on the side.

As the project dragged on, Eliza and I agreed to dedicate more time to get it moving. Eliza did her part, but again and again, my other obligations took precedence and I failed to do mine. One of the hardest conversations I've ever had was with Eliza when she rightfully questioned my commitment to our project. I had reached out to her with the initial concept, but Eliza had taken ownership in a way that far exceeded my expectations. My previous forays into start-ups had always been with a partner who was as part-time as I was or with multiple people who could take up any of my slack.

I'd prided myself on my ability to do so many things well, and I excused missed deadlines as acceptable because my quality of work was good. Turns out, not only was I the jerk in the business relationship, I had failed to tend to my friendship. Luckily, Eliza and I had a true bond and a lot of trust. During a series of e-mails and calls, she pointed out areas where I hadn't held up my obligations. The conversations also allowed me to express frustrations with our different communication styles, and we found differences we'd never noticed before we started working together.

Her candor also made me reexamine my earlier ventures, and I admit to having some shame in how I leaned too heavily on my partners without checking in and verifying that I was doing my part. I had good reasons for my behavior, but no reason can excuse poor treatment of others, regardless of whether they call you out or not. I can't reverse time; however, I have been more attentive and diligent to the needs of those around me, which improves who I am.

To be effective, we have to admit that we make mistakes and that we might accidentally sacrifice people and relationships, when we think it's only our needs that are in jeopardy. We lose friendships, mangle romantic relationships, hurt our families and ourselves. It's going to happen. Instead of pretending it won't or driving ourselves to dust to prevent it (that method won't work, by the way), we have to act smart and be honest with ourselves and those closest to us about the demands on our time and our psyches. We can't do it all, but we can do much more than we expect.

Last, I've found that self-care is a secret weapon at not losing Work-Life Jenga. I also admit, I am terrible at this. I can recite the benefits of exercise and the dangers of overwork. Yet I have a long list of excuses for why my treadmill sits unused. In a similar vein, I haven't taken a vacation in three years, which doesn't sound all that bad until I confess that the one before that took place seven years earlier.

My sister Leslie, the judge, was appointed at the age of thirty-nine and is one of the brightest legal minds of her time. She's also a Yale Law School alumna, and she's the first African American woman to become a federal judge in Georgia. I respect Leslie's legal acumen and her stellar résumé. Yet I stand in awe of Leslie's dedication to self-care. I'm not being facetious here. Women, especially black women, are notoriously bad at giving sufficient attention to our need for relaxation and respite from the daily grind of our obligations.

Leslie schedules her time off as deliberately as she plans a trial calendar, understanding how critically both must be treated. I have not yet gotten the hang of the vacation, though I do grant myself respites where I turn off my brain and allow my thoughts to recharge. We are doomed to burnout if we fail to incorporate time for hobbies or just doing nothing.

During my junior year of college, Spelman got a new dean of students. We'd chatted on occasion, as she served as the adviser to the SGA, where I then served as vice president. One day, she declared all classes canceled in recognition of the Day of Meta-noia. The literal translation of "metanoia" is a transformative change of heart. As happy as I was to have a day off from classes, I wondered why the dean did it. "You need to spend time with yourself," she warned me, sharing with me even back then that black women too often failed to give themselves moments of joy, and to find quiet spaces for reflection and renewal. For the record, I have found that men of color are often terrible at all of this too.

I wholly understand the trepidation some of us have when it comes to relaxation (I feel it too). It's like we're speeding ahead and being told to tap the brakes. Instead, consider self-care a pit stop on the racetrack. We all need tune-ups—physical, mental, and emotional. Since starting this book, I have downloaded an app to teach me guided meditations. I haven't achieved the level of consistency I'd like, and I fear my meditations will end up in the virtual graveyard with my yoga instruction and Couch to 5K plans. But it's a start, and it's something just for me.

Through meditation and other conscious acts, I am slowly incorporating changes into my daily routine to give space to my mind as I move through the most daunting challenge I've ever faced. We all pride ourselves on powering through because we don't want to be perceived as slackers or as weak. Many of us come from families or communities where self-care is a luxury. But we can start small, forgoing (for now) the weeklong vacation or regular hobby but committing to the act of daily personal analysis and taking a break a few times a day. Perhaps start with cutting out to go home and watch television—whatever show makes you happy. Maybe it means forgoing a Need to Do issue to keep your dinner and drinks reservation with friends. Visit a relative, or use a Groupon to find an activity you've long delayed doing. Bake for yourself, or order in instead of cooking for your family. Go for a walk for no reason at all with no discernible destination. Whatever your activity of choice, manage your time to allocate some to your well-being. And trust that self-care is a critical step on the road to world domination.

Work-Life Jenga gives us permission to be leaders, to be aggressive, and to be *human*. We pick our pieces and arrange our lives to suit the desires of our hearts, not the dictates of those around us. I realize that's easier said than done, just like taking a vacation, saying no to a friend or colleague, or working out at four thirty in the morning. But the way to win is to *try*.

PUTTING FIRST THINGS FIRST

To win at Work-Life Jenga, identify the priorities and concerns where you intend to focus your energy.

1. Imagine you are a reporter for the community newspaper. You have the job of creating headlines for the paper, and your life is the topic. Headlines should be no more than ten to fifteen words long and should give the reader a good sense of what the story would be about.

   A. Write the newspaper headline about you in three to five years.

      Personally:

      Professionally:

      In the Community:

   B. Write the newspaper headline about you in seven to ten years.

      Personally:

      Professionally:

      In the Community:

2. Write the title of your keynote address to the senior class of your high school in twenty-five years.

3. You've been awarded a Nobel Prize. What field? For what achievement?

4. You have solved one major crisis (in your family, in your field, in your community, in the world). What was it? How did you do it?

5. What would you do if you had two more useful hours in the day?

Nine

TAKING POWER

I began writing this book to give potential minority leaders some answers on how to be successful and to show what I've done—wrong or right—on my own journey. To write honestly and practically about how the lessons of otherness start early and leave indelible marks because I know they shake our confidence, stifle our ambition, and undermine our sense of possibility. Despite my accomplishments, every once in a while a single article or a nasty reader comment about my hairstyle or my skin color can spin my self-assurance into second thoughts. They never last long, but the fact that I still grapple with doubt about my rightness to be where I am proves how resilient these experiences can be.

Of course, not all setbacks and challenges are rooted in discrimination, but these experiences affect our thinking about the world and about ourselves; and they temper how we respond to opportunity and adversity. We might learn to assume the worst, and understandably so. When we buck against the conventional wisdom, we can be charged with being too disruptive or problematic. And with the absence of role models to show us the way, we are left with our own narrow experiences as guides.

My campaign for governor has illuminated issues I hadn't fully considered and still cannot completely articulate. Positions I have long held now get filtered through lenses I don't recognize, the tinge of race and gender distorting what I say and do. I spoke recently to a community group about criminal justice reform, a passion of mine. After my talk, an older white gentleman came up to me and asked if I'd be willing to help his son too, or if my plans were only for black men in jail. Taken aback, I replayed my speech in my head, trying to figure out if I had somehow signaled that I would help *only* my own racial group. Still, I assured him my policies encompassed anyone in the system and that I had been working closely with the Republican governor on the issues. I invoked the governor to give him comfort that I'd worked with white leaders on these policies, to allay his fears. In politics, this situation isn't unexpected, but it remains disconcerting. From my background to my vision, I have to navigate verbal cues to explain my mission to serve all while acknowledging the specific barriers to minority communities. But I've gotten pretty good at it, as have many of you.

In the end, the point of this book is to help you get even better at it. To ask each of us to think about *why* we want what we want and to give ourselves permission to figure out *how* we can continue to grow personally and professionally. I want you to be uncomfortable with the exercises, to dig into your plans, and to question your assumptions about what could be yours. My mission is to help you imagine or reimagine your future. Whether you're a college student fretting over changing your major, or a nurse who wants to start a bakery, or a frustrated parent who plans to run for the school board, I am talking to you. A lot of you reading this have probably already charted some path and no doubt can offer many examples of your successes. For you, I intend to nudge you to think critically about where you are now and where you desire to go next—and I want to remind you to never be ashamed of reaching for more, wherever it resides. For all of us, even me, we have to consistently remember that the game is stacked, but if we can unlock the cheat codes, we can play to win. We *can* take power.

The lesson of taking power lies in how we do things, how we see our roles in the world we wish to create. Real leadership, true power, understands how to enter the world purposefully and knows what we're responsible for doing here. To take power is to use the best of what resides within us for sketching a vision for the future, written large or small. Power requires a conscious effort on our part to move our own lives to where we want them to be, because we've got to move against what historically has been defined as the way we *should* live our lives or inhabit this space.

Taking power does not mean that you always do something huge. Part of being a leader is recognizing that whatever your corner of the world, whatever small piece you happen to be able to touch, that power should make you move it a little bit. And it doesn't have to be about big life-altering news or headline-grabbing decisions. It is correcting yourself when you decline a chance to advance. Instead of slogging through a job you merely tolerate, it's taking a class about how to turn your hobby into a side hustle.

Taking power demands self-analysis. You should regularly

202 LEAD FROM THE OUTSIDE

challenge yourself to do more, to be more, to examine your
life and the world around you. Then endeavor to make modest
improvements, knowing that, together, those incremental changes
alter perceptions and then reality. Raise your hand in a meeting
and share your brainstorm. Talk to a stranger on the elevator.
Accept a compliment without flinching or apologizing. Take
credit for an idea you've had—don't deflect or pretend false mod-
esty. Stretch yourself to be the leader you imagine. Be one who
places her sense of self above fears of humiliation or chagrin.

If we take ownership of our identities and leverage our capacity
to lead, we will make waves and headlines and enemies. Change
is disruptive, uncomfortable, and inevitable, but we are each
responsible for shaping the direction of new power. What began
for me as a compelling project to inspire and harness the talent
of potential minority leaders is now a call to arms. We stand in a
historical moment, one that demands revolutionary leadership.
Regardless of the scale of action, our collective mission is to
expand the image of leadership across a diverse coalition of races,
faiths, statuses, and socioeconomic backgrounds. But we can't do
it alone, nor should we. Change in power needs allies, and those
of us preparing to lead will face critiques from both outside and
within our circles and communities.

   In 2017, *Cosmopolitan* published a profile on my bid for governor, and the reporter began her piece with a provocative opening. "If all goes as planned, the earliest Stacey Abrams would run
for president is in 2028. Not 2020—that's too soon. Not 2024—
the Democrat who vanquishes President Trump in 2020 will
be up for reelection. No, the first opportunity is 2028. That's
her year."

During our interview, I'd mentioned my life-planning spread-sheet to the reporter, Rebecca Nelson, and she latched on to the idea, asking about the highest office to which I aspired. Politics 101 says never admit to wanting to be president. You can specu-late about any other office, any other ambition, but the presidency is forbidden. The sheer gall of speaking the goal aloud suppos-edly reeks of opportunism, or, as the Republican Governors Association posted in a tweet the next day, aspiring so high is "bizarre." In my orbit, folks flinched in dismay at my bald hon-esty. *Why would you say that?*

When Ms. Nelson asked me, I had indeed hesitated about answering. I could spin the response, reassuring her and her read-ers of my solitary commitment to become governor of Georgia, but she knew that—it's why she was talking to me in the first place. I could pivot, redirect her from the spreadsheet, which could seem calculating to those who didn't understand it as a tool I'd been using since college to help me dissect big goals. Or, I could be forthright, cutting through the code of silence that held women and people of color back from staking a claim on simply the right to think about running for our nation's highest post. As I explained to the reporter, my mission is to tackle poverty and its myriad drains on our society. The governor of Georgia can do much to address the issue in my home state; imagine what successful, proven policies can do on a national level. The only job I know of with that kind of reach is the president of the United States, the hardest job in the world to get. So, if I want to accom-plish my mission, I need to be thinking about how to get to that post. We admire the guy in the mailroom who plots to become the CEO but scoff at the woman who says she wants the same.

Our team prepared for the barrage of criticism to come when the article went live, and it certainly came. Then a funny thing happened. First, Karen Finney, a seasoned political communications director and top aide to Hillary Clinton, replied to the RGA, "Shame on the RGA—you're basically saying young women and girls shouldn't have goals and aspirations! Why ok for men not women?" Then came philanthropist Barbara Lee to my defense: "Her ambition (and compassion) should be lauded, not derided." EMILY's List sent in the troops: "And here's the RGA proving her point that people will use a narrative that women are too ambitious to tear down women of color." And on and on it went that day, drowning out the criticism, affirming the validity of speaking plans into existence, an army of allies to my defense. Without my asking for the help. Without a plea for support. In a microcultural moment, women of every stripe—and some men—stepped up and demanded that the RGA back down. And, for the day, they did.

In a book focused on minority identities, now seems an important time to remind us all that we can't do this alone. Allyship speaks to a willingness to fight for equality on behalf of marginalized groups of which you are not a part. Knowing how to do so, though, can be hard. Conversations abound about being an effective ally, and we should welcome the awkward discussions. The shift in our cultural norms excites me, not simply because of the greater awareness of the barriers faced by those *not* born to power but because more and more people see that they have an active role to play in destroying those obstacles. The strongest ally understands his or her privilege—that is to say, the ability to make choices not grounded in a specific identity. Basically, a good ally consciously accepts that there are experiences you cannot understand, despite a sense of empathy.

And let's not forget, privilege exists even within those who are encompassed by a minority identity. I recently gave a speech to the Lesbians Who Tech conference about the responsibility of straight allies, about how we should be held to account in politics. The crux of my talk focused on how the LGBTQ+ community could train us to be better allies, to know that some experiences are beyond our ken. I learned how to be a better ally from my friends Simone and Sam, who individually operated as people of color in the LGBTQ+ community but from starkly distinct vantage points. Simone, a black lesbian in her forties, and Sam, an openly gay millennial Korean American, both served in the state legislature, proving that no one operates on solely one identity. The best allies own their privilege not as a badge of honor but as a reminder to be constantly listening and learning to become better at offering support to others.

There's a colloquialism I've embraced: let your haters be your motivators. If we attempt to be more than prescribed by our demographics, we will face opposition, not just the nasty trolls of the Internet, who nitpick at superficial differences or double-down on rhetoric to undermine confidence. I'm talking about the more insidious, effective acts of sabotage that make you question whether the goal is worth the pain. From whisper campaigns to outright hostility, any progress could draw detractors and those who feel threatened. Power, in some instances, is absolutely a zero-sum affair, and your victory inherently means another's defeat. Good leaders do not ignore this consequence; they measure the loss to others and the harm to themselves and their objectives. If the goal is worth it, we must stay the course and not fall prey to the insults, however caustic and demeaning. I'm not allowed to read the comment section of our local newspaper online and my team steers me away from Facebook other than

206 LEAD FROM THE OUTSIDE

official posts. Occasionally, I let my curiosity get the better of me, but I have realized that never leans to my benefit.

History is littered with stories of naysayers who decry new-comers and excoriate innovators. Human nature often turns us away from what hasn't yet been tried—even if we come to regret it later. Remember this, however, in the darkest moments, when the work doesn't seem worth it, and change seems just out of reach: out of our willingness to push through comes a tremendous power. We use the fire of our passions and the angst of our opposition to push past the boundaries of what we expect of ourselves and what the world expects of us. We can harness this energy to lead from the outside and make real change. This is our power. We are entitled. So use it.

STACEY'S AMBITION SPREADSHEET

Use this tool to remind you why you want what you want and what you need to get there.

Ambition:_____

GOAL	RATIONALE	STRATEGIES	RESOURCES	TIMELINE
(what do you want?)	(why do you want it?)	(what should you do?)	(whose help do you need . . . and what help do you need?)	(when should each step be done?)

ACKNOWLEDGMENTS

When you write a book that is part memoir, part advice, and part alchemy, the list of those who deserve credit grows exponentially. I am deeply grateful to the people who have helped me grow in my careers, who have advised me, and the ones who let me practice my advice on them.

Family always comes first. To my mother and father, the Reverends Carolyn and Robert Abrams, I am profoundly grateful. As my mom has said a time or two, I was in a hurry to get into the world, so much so that she had to be on bed rest for two months. Once I made my arrival, my parents raised me with a boundless belief in my potential, anchored by a sense of responsibility to others. My first teachers, they gave me a love of words and a gift for storytelling. I like to think I am a blend of my parents: Dad's indignation at inaction and his determination, Mom's compassion and her patience, knowing folks will come around. I admire their lived passion for justice and wry humor about a world that could cause permanent bitterness. And when my mistakes grew heavy and painful, they wrapped me in love and forgiveness and hope. No one will ever know finer people than my parents, and I give thanks daily for my great fortune to be born into their care.

Dr. Andrea Abrams, my eldest sister and second teacher, has been my confidant and my protector—the leader of a rowdy tribe of siblings who still look to her for guidance, comfort, and intercession with our parents. Whether she's fending off the bully on the school bus or smartly editing this book's draft proposal, Andrea is there, as she has been my entire life—sometimes standing in front of me, and never out of reach. Her emotional clarity weaves through my logic, lighting ideas I may have missed. Her generosity of time allows me to pack more into my own days. With her as my lodestar, I will always find my way.

My sister, Judge Leslie Abrams, showed up in my life eleven months and twenty-seven days after my arrival, and I thank God for the precious gift of a friend and collaborator who gives yin to my yang. She kept my secrets in childhood and my dreams of the future. Leslie edited my first book, her sharp sense of narrative aiding me more than she will know. She is possessed of a moral core that consistently challenges me to be better and kinder, and her joie de vivre lifts me up and makes me smile with my whole heart.

My gratitude to Richard Abrams, my brother, for his example of strength, and his resilience in the face of difficulties. I have watched him overcome obstacles from his earliest days that would crush weaker men. Instead, he fought his way through with a sly smile and a keen intelligence I continue to admire. His quiet ways do not hide his spirit, and he has never failed to step up when I call. I am proud of the man he is and continues to become. Watching him raise Jorden, Riyan, and Ayren with his wife, Nakia, I see the wonders of family serve a new generation.

During his matriculation at Morehouse College, my brother Walter shared my apartment and my many lives as attorney, activist, and writer. When I shoved the pages of my second novel in front of him, he didn't balk or mock my request. Nope, he read his first romance novel and gave me excellent feedback. In Walter, I have a sparring partner, a cheerleader, and an early morning call on every birthday. I am grateful for his loyalty and his brilliance, and for his determination to try and get it right.

When you are the last of a set, it would be easy to go unnoticed. For my youngest sister, Dr. Audrey Jeanine Abrams-McLean, that was never an option. Jeanine stuns me time and again with her courage—the willingness to be herself, unapologetically, authentically, and brazenly. She is wicked smart, brusquely sweet, invariably hilarious, and a perfect antidote to days when I wrestle with my choices and need a listening ear and open heart. Her example as wife to Brandon and mother to Cameron and Devin evokes only joy. Though youngest, she has an old soul and a wisdom that humbles me. Though last, she has never been far behind, and somehow manages to get places first. She read this manuscript in its raw form, and her advice has made this a stronger work.

My niece, Faith, allowed me to share her story in these pages, a brave act for an eleven-year-old. I am honored by her courage, and I am delighted by the chance to watch her grow and mature. She binds our family tighter, a unique link between my parents, my siblings, and her cousins, and I adore her.

For my extended family, additional thanks to my brother-in-law Brandon, who shared his house during my extended stay and offered his constant support during everything; my sister-in-law

Nakia, who shows up, no questions asked, and lets me borrow her children for necessary hugs; and my other nieces and nephews, Jorden (of video games and thoughtful questions), Cameron (of inquisitive mind and clever words), Riyan (of quiet intelligence and keen eyes), Ayren (of sweet smiles and belly laughs), and Devin (of dynamo speed and infectious giggles). And to my grandmother, Wilter Abrams, who begs me to slow down but never fails to urge me on.

One perk of humanity is the ability to make friends into more, to learn from them and to disappoint without losing their love. Archimedes said, "Give me a place to stand, and I will move the earth." I offer this modification: "Give me good friends to stand beside, and we will move the world."

Thank you to my first Spelman sisters, the late, beloved Michelle Slater, Reena Wyatt, Edana Walker, Ayanay Ferguson, Mendi Lewis, Alyson Jones, Renee Page, Rimani Kelsey, Caryn Johnson, Letricia Henson, Janet Scott, and those also who lifted me up and whose names are etched in my heart. And to Camille Johnson, who has been my friend since the first week of college, riding shotgun on every election I have ever waged, thank you for hard questions and an unquestioning willingness to act first and recriminate later.

Dr. Johnnetta B. Cole, my adored Dr. C, thank you for the time at your kitchen island at Spelman, at your office desk on Beechwood Avenue, in your sunroom in Greensboro, and in your life since 1991. Through you, I honed my capacity to tell stories through speeches, to speak truth to power, and to ask for what I needed from those who could provide.

My extended Truman Scholarship family contributed to this book by helping shape me in their ways: Louis Blair, who handed me a roadmap to places I had never imagined; Eliza Leighton, who loves more generously than anyone deserves and is friend, business partner, and instigator; Gregg Behr, who has crappy taste in college football but is an extraordinary man and thought leader; Maggie Church, who will never allow time to eclipse the heart; Stacey Brandenburg, a shared name, a beautiful soul, and stories we will never tell; Meredith Moss, a woman of spirit deserving of all the best; Tara Kneller Yglesias, a leader who never allows dictates to dictate her fortunes; Andrew Rich and Tonji Wade, who keep the Truman legacy alive; Max (and Kate) Finberg, who make the world better each day; Diana McAdoo, who is clever and kind and a monthly reminder on my phone to smile; and Brooks Allen, who followed me from Truman to Yale but is always ahead of me when it matters. I am also beholden to senior scholars U.S. Senator Chris Coons, U.S. Attorney Bill Mercer, Margot Rogers, Brother Rogers, and Mary Tolar, who helped fix my lens upon the world, and those fellow Trumans who allowed me to grill them or stand with them in Uncle Harry's name.

Pai-Ling Yin was my roommate of chance in a dorm in Liberty, Missouri, and my roommate of choice in a dorm in Washington, D.C. When I tell my stories, she is woven throughout the pages, a voice of unwavering belief in my capacity, an unexpected kindness in my moments of worry. I share with her a friendship that has stretched across years, oceans and, if Anne Rice is to be believed, lifetimes. My personal profountain (not a typo), she is all.

Will Dobson sees in me truths I cannot, even when I squint. He hears in my ideas the pathways to dreams I didn't know I had. Through his urging, I investigated a broader world and found in myself a complexity I might have missed without his ceaseless prodding. He is consigliere, crucible, voice of reason, compass, and a damned fine editor. Most importantly, Will is and ever will be my dear, true friend.

For this book, I drew on the stories and relationships that have shaped who I am and how I see the world. Allegra Lawrence-Hardy, who preceded me at Spelman College and Yale Law School, and whose legend is never overstated, has been a sounding board and ally across my many different lives. As I reach for more, she lifts me up. Teresa Wynn Roseborough dared me to imagine possibilities I scarcely believed real, and I am thankful for her belief in my potential. Lara O'Connor Hodgson has been a partner in business and a friend in every way that counts. Our conversation in a lunch line transformed and extended my worldview, and our plotting over her dining-room table taught me more than I can express. Lisa Borders has been my running buddy and cheerful confederate in our plans to do a whole bunch. Monika Majors and Che Watkins inspired me to wage a different kind of campaign in 2006, and I remain grateful for the support. Morgan Smith and Kathy Betty both run faster but let me keep up. Ingrid Fisher clears a space for my writings and ramblings. John Hayes and Archie Jones gave me room to lead. And Ben Jealous, who is running his own race, has been in league with me for more than two decades—and I pray for many more.

I must also thank the LBJ School of Public Affairs and Dean Max Sherman, who nudged me to leap. And I am obliged to Yale Law School, my classmates and professors, who gave me a place to land.

My tenure at the City of Atlanta trained me to understand the intersection of government and leadership. I appreciate the tutelage of Mayor Shirley Franklin, Linda DiSantis, Greg Giornelli, Roz Newell, and Laurette Woods, and the whole company of the Law Department and my clients.

With gratitude to Whip Carolyn Hugley and Representative Al Williams, who sat beside me during my time at the Capitol, offered counsel whether I asked or not, listened as I searched for answers, then pretended I'd found them. I am also indebted to the members of the Georgia General Assembly and the second floor for the tutelage, patience, and grace as we worked for a stronger Georgia.

Leadership requires having someone willing to come along on the journey. The Georgia House Democratic Caucus leadership team (Genny Castillo, Brooks Emanuel, Buck Fleming, Liz Flowers, Howard Franklin, Fal Hindash, Brian Harkins, Sarah Henderson, Salena Jegede, DeAndre Jones, Erin Kadzis, Justin Kirnon, Sophie Loghman, Priyanka Mantha, Carolyn Monden, Emily Oh, Ashley Robinson, Jaiah Scott, Robert Sills, Celina Stewart, Craig Walters, Jonae Wartel, and Don Weigel) and my legislative aides taught me how to be a better, more thoughtful boss as they grew into tremendous leaders in their own rights.

Thank you to the labor unions of Georgia that invested in my vision and defended our values, with special thank-yous to Mitchell Byrd, Charlie Fleming, Steve Lomax, Kenny Mullins, Ben Myers, Tracey-Ann Nelson, Gene O'Kelley, Yvonne Robinson, Dorothy Townsend, Mary Lou Waymer, and Sherilyn Wright. And the Democratic Legislative Campaign Committee, which believed me when I said minority party was shorthand for opportunity. I appreciate the hard work of DuBose Porter, Rebecca DeHart, and the Georgia Democratic Party. I am buoyed daily by the support of EMILY's List, Higher Heights for America, and a host of others. So much of my work would not have been possible without Steve Phillips and Susan Sandler, Michael Vachon and the Soros family, Eddy Morales, and others who shared my vision for a democracy made more diverse. To the allies and warriors of the New Georgia Project, here and around the country, I hold you in the highest regard and esteem. And I am humbled by the constituents of Georgia House District 84 turned 89; thank you for allowing me eleven years of service on your behalf.

I can think of few finer moments than when those you lead become those you turn to for advice and whose stories have entered these pages, and so I offer my sincerest gratitude to Brandon Evans for his candor, stratagems, and his confidence in half-formed notions and risky endeavors; Ashley Robinson, for her bold determination, wild ideas, and her unwavering belief that we'll get there; Genny Castillo for her effervescence and groundedness; and Justin Kirnon for his steady, complex view of the possible.

The highest test of leadership I have faced comes with my bid for governor of Georgia. I do not travel this campaign alone, as I am surrounded by Team Abrams—the Abrams for Governor campaign staff, who astound me daily with their ingenuity and industry, and the volunteers and supporters who lift up this vision for all to see.

Finding the words to write this book would not have been possible without the careful eyes of Priyanka Mantha, who read both proposal and manuscript with care and thoughtfulness, and whose quick mind challenges me and makes me sharper. Chelsey Hall, an accidental editor, sits with me each day on this campaign and has been an enthusiastic vetter of ideas. Her feedback refined my efforts and improved each page, and I cannot thank her enough.

Kelly Cole used the incisive mind and quiet generosity I so genuinely admire and respect in her thoughtful reading of multiple proposal drafts, and she gave me guideposts for improving its direction. But I am most grateful for her unexpected email in late 2016 about why now was the time to put this book into motion, words that have spurred me on when I might have hesitated.

Lauren Groh-Wargo has been my political partner, a dynamic and astute leader, and a master strategist who would give Clausewitz pause. Her fine, noble actions speak louder than any words, and her honesty in friendship has smoothed the roughest roads. I am extremely lucky to have been connected to her, to fight beside her, and to join with her in the constant pursuit of good. She makes daring the impossible fun.

I began writing this book in 2014, after a conversation with Will Lippincott, who warned me that to offer my advice, I would have to tell my own story. I balked at the notion, but he made too much sense. Although he left the world of author representation for broader publication, his thoughtful, probing questions shaped this idea into a book I am proud to have written.

Rebecca Traister interviewed me for an article, and in the process, we got to talking about the art of writing. I shared my trepidation about penning something so revelatory at a time when I was also thinking about running for governor. As is her way, she offered fresh perspectives I hadn't considered, and I thank her for the probing questions and sympathetic input. Then she introduced me to my agent.

My literary agent, Linda Loewenthal, and her team adapted to absurd timetables, a hardheaded writer with privacy issues, and a concept that had its challenges, and for her efforts, I can now thank her for a work I hope will do her proud. Thank you for the quick turnarounds, for the healthy challenges to my ego and my writing style, and for bringing me to a publishing house that understood my goals.

Henry Holt and Company has an extraordinary roster of authors, and I will never forget sitting around a conference table in July, with Steve Rubin, Maggie Richards, Gillian Blake, and Libby Burton, my soon-to-be editor. I remain grateful for their enthusiasm and conviction. Thank you also to Carolyn O'Keefe and Hannah Campbell, and the entire Holt team. Libby has my deepest gratitude for accommodating a compressed timeline, a crazy campaign schedule, and for moving this from proposal to final edits at an inhuman speed. I appreciate her calm in the face of missed deadlines, and her faith that I really could get this done and run for office. Thank you for making this work.

INDEX

abolitionism, 24

Abrams, Dr. Andrea, xxii, 45–46, 109, 180

Abrams, Carolyn, xix, xxi–xxiii, xxv, 8, 9, 12, 14, 31, 56–58, 104, 109, 111–12, 131, 133–34, 168, 176–77

Abrams, Faith, 111–12, 176–77, 178, 211

Abrams, Leslie, xxii, 109, 180, 193

Abrams, Richard, xxii, 110, 179–80

Abrams, Robert, xix, xxi–xxiii, 8, 31, 56–58, 104, 109, 111–12, 128, 133–34, 176–77

Abrams, Walter, xv, xvi, xxii, 111–12, 176, 178, 179–80

Abrams-McLean, Dr. Audrey Jeanine, xxii, 131, 179

Abzug, Bella, 58

access and entry, gaining, 59–65

accolades, 75–76, 151

action, ambition turned into, 3–27

adviser, 86–88, 92, 94, 101, 102

affirmative action, 62, 72

Affordable Care Act, 136–37

age and ageism, xxvi, 76, 169, 170, 181

AIDS, 47

Airbnb, 114

allies, 204–5

Alstott, Anne, 5

Alstott's Queries, 5, 6, 10

Alvarado, Linda, 58

ambition, 3–27, 122, 181, 191, 199
    exercise, 26–27
    spreadsheet, 207
    turned into action, 3–27

anger, 20, 188

apartheid, 16

Aquafina, 157

Aristotle, *Poetics*, 89

Arizona, 142

arrogance, 80

arts, 24

Asian Americans, xiii

Atlanta, xxvi, 13, 15–22, 25, 33, 64, 66, 68, 79, 88, 138, 146, 163, 176, 177, 178
    Abrams as deputy city attorney for, 79–82, 164
    Office of Youth Services, 21

Atlanta BeltLine, Inc., 91
Atlanta University Center, 16–17
Atlantic, The, 116
authenticity, 33, 35, 44–46, 155

balance, myth of, 175–76, 183
Banneker, Benjamin, 24
bar exam, 110
basketball, 177–78
being wrong, 145–48, 150
beliefs, 170–72
Bell, Simone, 46–48
Beyoncé, 24
Blakely, Sara, 159
BLUE Institute, 155
board of advisers, 92–96, 101–2
boldness, 136–41
Booker, Johnnie, 68–69
Borders, Lisa, 177–78
bottled water, 142, 157, 165
building networks, 92–96
bullying, 47
Burns, Robert, 76
business, xvi, 2, 5, 6, 22, 34, 134
    building networks, 92–96
    discrimination, 34–35
    failure and, 131–50
    fund-raising, 122–28
    gaining access and entry, 59–65
    mentors and, 79–103
    money matters and, 103–30
    moving up, 65–70
    opportunity and, 53–78
    power and, 151–74
    taking power, 199–206
    titles, 161–62
    Work-Life Jenga and, 175–97
BuzzFeed, 83

career, 22–25, 30
    building networks, 92–96
    entrepreneurship, 34–35, 77,
        90–91, 107, 114, 125, 127,
        142–43, 158–59, 161–63, 186–87
    failure and, 131–50
    gaining access and entry, 59–65
    management style, 79–84
    mentors and, 79–103

money matters and, 103–30
    moving up, 65–70
    opportunity and, 53–78
    power and, 151–74
    side hustle, 114, 201
    taking power, 199–206
    Work-Life Jenga and, 175–97
Castillo, Genny, 63–64
caution, 133–36
changing the rules of engagement,
    165–70
children, 1–2, 3, 115, 125, 165, 176,
    179, 180, 181
civil rights movement, xxiii, 16, 156
Clark, Brandy, "Pray to Jesus," 103–4
Clark Atlanta University, 16
class, xiv, xvii, 2, 4, 23, 76
Cleage, Pearl, 89
Clearpoint.org, 114
Clinton, Bill, 181
Clinton, Hillary, xiii, 181, 204
Coates, Ta-Nehisi, "The Case for
    Reparations," 116
Coca-Cola, 157
Cole, Dr. Johnnetta, 93–94, 100, 118,
    120
collaboration, 155, 169
college, xxi, xxii, xxiii–xxiv, xxvi,
    1–2, 9–10, 11–14, 15–16, 21,
    30, 37–38, 45, 57, 61, 73, 75,
    93, 103–5, 112, 140, 180, 181,
    189–90, 193–94, 200
    affirmative action, 62
    black, 9–18
    debt, xvi, 107–18
    economic success and, 104–5
    "legacy" admissions, 62
    scholarships, 104–5, 108, 109, 118,
        140
    tuition hikes, 117–21
    See also specific colleges
concession, xi, xiii–xv, xvii
confidence, xxvii, xxviii, 8, 11, 13
Congress, 58, 59
Constitution, U.S., xiv
construction, 106
Consumer Credit Counseling, 114
Cosmopolitan, 202

credit, 106
 cards, 108–9, 113, 114
 college debt, 107–18
 counseling, 114–15
 denial of, 106
 FICO score, 109, 110
 report, 110, 115
crime, 2
C-SPAN, 40, 70

Dasani, 157
Davis, Wendy, 156–57
day care, 2
Deal, Nathan, 140
debt, xv, xvi, 106
 college, xvi, 107–18
 credit card, 108–9, 113, 114
 getting out of, 113–17
 side hustle and, 114
democracy, xvi
Democratic National Convention
 (1964), 156
Democratic Party, xi, xii, xiii, 39–43,
 54, 62, 63, 66, 88, 136–37, 140, 141,
 152–53, 156, 159, 164, 167, 169, 202
DiSantis, Linda, 138–39
discrimination, 199
 business, 34–35
 gender, xxi, xxvi, 31, 34, 38,
  40–48, 61, 74–75, 95–96, 106,
  116, 158, 200, 203–4
 money, 57–58, 106, 116
 political, 40–43, 46–48, 54–55, 61,
  73, 106, 167, 200, 203–4
 racial, xxiii, xxvi, 15–22, 40–48,
  57–58, 61, 74–75, 106, 116, 200
 sexual orientation, 46–48
double standard, 74–75
doubt, 70–74
drug addiction, xxviii, 20, 112, 176
dyslexia, 57

Ebay, 114
Edelman, Marian Wright, 16
education, xxi, xxiii, 1–2, 7–10, 57,
 104, 140
 debt, 107–18
 economic success and, 104–5

letting your light shine, 133–34
 See also college
Eisenhower, Dwight D., 183, 184
election process, unfairness of, xi,
 xiii–xvii
Eliot, George, 157–58
embracing failure, 141–45
EMILY's List, 77, 204
endorsements, 66, 151
entrepreneurship, xii, 34–35, 77,
 90–91, 107, 114, 125, 127,
 142–43, 158–59, 161–63, 186–87
Evans, Brandon, 67
exercise, 193, 194

Facebook, 205–6
fail forward, 143
failure, xv, xviii, 30, 42, 131–50,
 158–59
 best way to be wrong, 145–48, 150
 boldness and, 136–41
 embracing, 141–45
 flying and, 141–45
 holding yourself back, 133–36
fairy godmother experience, 26
false sense of leadership, 163–64
family, 2, 98, 176–77, 178, 179–81,
 184, 191, 192, 194
family leave, 47
Family Room app, 191–92
fear, 4, 6, 9, 18, 29–51, 77, 119, 127, 132
 as a friend, 36–39
 name it and know it, 32–36
 stereotypes and, 32–48
 used as fuel, 39–49
feedback, 98–99
FEMA, 176
FICO score, 109, 110
fiction writing, xxvi, 12, 13, 23,
 88–89, 114, 157–58, 180, 181–83
financial fluency, 117–21, 129–30
Finney, Karen, 204
firing employees, 81–82, 139, 186–87
first things first, 179–86, 196–97
flip-flopping, 171
Ford Foundation, xxiv
Fortune 500, 68, 134
Franklin, Shirley, 88, 138, 146

fund-raising, 66, 93, 106, 107, 120, 122–28, 130, 151–52, 164–65

gaining access and entry, 59–65
gangs, 20
gender, xii, xiii, xiv, xvii, xx, xxiv, xxv, xxvi, 4, 6, 13, 58, 76, 134, 136, 203
   discrimination, xxi, xxvi, 31, 34, 37, 38, 40–48, 61, 74–75, 95–96, 106, 116, 158, 200, 203–4
   expectations, 181
   stereotypes, 9, 10, 12, 36, 39, 41–48
generosity, 99
Georgia, xxvi–xxvii, 1–25, 33, 53–55, 104, 136–37, 178, 193
   Abrams's campaign for governor, xi–xviii, xxvii, 2, 23, 31–32, 43, 68, 140, 190, 200, 203
   aftermath of 2018 gubernatorial election, xi–xviii
   redistricting maps, xii
   voter registration, 53–55
Georgia House of Representatives, xxvi, 39–40, 46–48, 65–70, 136–37, 140, 152–53, 159–60, 191
   Abrams as minority leader, 39–43, 62–64, 69–70, 126, 140, 160, 165
   Crossover Day, 152–53
getting lost in possibilities, 5–7
getting out of debt, 113–17
Girl Scouts, 128
GoFundMe, 122
Gotta Do, 184
Great Recession, 47, 140
Groh-Wargo, Lauren, 53, 190
Groupon, 194
guerrilla tactics, 160

H. A. Brown Memorial United Methodist Church, 176
hacking, 53–78
Hamer, Fannie Lou, 156
happiness, 188, 194
Hayes, John, 142
health care, 136–37, 177, 188
Higher Heights for America, 77

Hodgson, Lara, 90, 91, 92, 142, 157, 148, 161, 162, 165, 177, 178, 186, 187
holding yourself back, 133–36
HOPE Scholarship, 140
Hugley, Carolyn, 88
humility, 71–73
Hurricane Katrina, 111, 176, 178

identity politics, 134
immigrants, xxix, 24
India, 24
informational meetings, 92
Insomnia Consulting, LLC, 91, 161–62, 186–87
interest rates, 110–11
Internet, 114, 205
internships, 63–64, 67, 165
intimacy, 98
IRS, 112, 143, 144
"it takes a village" theory, 100

Jackson, Maynard, 19–21
Jefferson, Thomas, 24
jerks, dealing with, 186–89
Johnson, Lyndon B., 156

Kentucky, 180
Kickstarter, 122
King, Martin Luther, Jr., 16
King, Rodney, 15–18, 20
Kitashima, Tsuyako "Sox," 58–59
Kroger, 142

labels, 161–62, 170
Latinos, xii
law, 5, 24–25, 79–82, 87–88, 108, 135, 138–39, 143–45, 164–65, 193
   mistakes, 143–45
   school, xxvi, 5, 107, 108, 109, 110, 131–32, 181, 193
leadership, xii, xiii, xv, xvii–xviii, xxvii–xxx
   failure and, 131–50
   false sense of, 163–64
   fear and, 30–51
   management style, 79–84
   mentors and, 79–103

money and, 103–30
opportunity and, 53–78
power and, 151–74
taking power, 199–206
wanting more, 1–27
Work-Life Jenga and, 175–97
Lee, Barbara, 204
"legacy" admissions, 62
Lesbians Who Tech, 61, 205
letting your light shine, 133–41
LGBTQ+ community, 39, 46–48,
   61, 136, 205
LinkedIn, 61
lobbyists, political, 147–48
Los Angeles, 15–16
love, 11–12, 14
Lowell, Elizabeth, xxvi

management style, 79–84
manufacturing, 106
mapping, power, 166–70, 173–74
marriage, 98, 179, 180, 181
   same-sex, 47
martyrdom, 187
Maxwell, Zerlina, 71
McDaniel, Allen, 118, 119, 120
meditation, 194
meekness, 133–36, 139
mentors, 79–103, 146
   adviser, 86–88, 92, 94, 101, 102
   building networks, 92–96
   help them help you, 96–100
   management style and, 79–84
   myth of, 79–103
   peer, 89–91, 93, 101
   situational, 85, 88–89, 101
   sponsor, 85–86, 101
   taxonomy, 84–91
Might Get Around To, 184, 185
Miranda, Lin-Manuel, 24
Mississippi, xix–xxv, xxvii, 3, 57, 104
Mississippi Freedom Democratic
   Party, 156
mistakes, 131–50, 192
money, 12, 13, 21, 22, 55–58, 89–90,
   103–30, 154, 155
   building everything from next to
      nothing, 121–28

college debt, 107–18
discrimination, 57–58, 106, 116
education and economic success,
   104–5
financial fluency, 117–21, 129–30
fund-raising, 6, 93, 106, 107, 120,
   122–28, 130, 151–52, 164–65
matters, 103–30
mistakes, 107–17
personal finances, 103–21, 129
resources, 129–30
wealth gaps, 103–4, 106, 115–16
Montgomery, Selena, 182
Morehouse College, 9, 16
Morris Brown College, 16
moving on up, 65–70
multiplier effect, 123
music, 24, 131–33, 181
Myers-Briggs type, 83
myth of balance, 175–76, 183

NAACP, 58
NASA Lunar Module, 187
Need to Do, 184–85, 194
Nelson, Rebecca, 203
networks, 92–96, 125, 127
   building, 92–96
New Georgia Project, 54–55
news media, 18–19, 41, 85–86
NGOs, 25
nonprofit organizations, 6, 25, 120,
   164, 168
Nourish, 91, 142, 143, 165
novels, writing, xxvi, 12, 13, 23,
   88–89, 114, 157–58, 180, 181–83,
   190, 191
NOW Corp., 91, 142–43, 191

Obama, Barack, xiii
old boys' club, 61
O'Neal, Shaquille, 91
opportunity, 53–78, 199
   gaining access and entry,
      59–65
   hacking and owning, 53–78
   moving on up, 65–70
   owning, 74–77
   taming self-doubt, 70–74

otherness, 29–51, 77, 199
  competition for primacy of, 47–48
  stereotypes and, 39–48
Oughta Do, 184, 185

Park, Sam, 136–37
peer mentor, 89–91, 93, 101
Pelosi, Nancy, 42
personal finances, 103–21, 129
personality tests, 83
personal relationships, 179–86, 192
police, and racism, 15–19
politics, xxvii, 2, 23, 31–32, 39–43,
    53–55, 61–70, 77, 87, 88, 91, 93,
    100, 121, 146–47, 156–57, 167,
    170–71, 179, 181, 190, 193, 200,
    202–4
  boldness and, 136–41
  concession, xi, xii–xv, xvii
  discrimination, 40–43, 46–48,
    54–55, 61, 73, 106, 167, 200,
    203–4
  fund-raising, 124–27, 164–65
  Georgia, xi–xviii, xxvi, 39–43,
    46–48, 53–55, 62–70, 79–82,
    126, 136–37, 140, 152–53,
    159–60, 165, 191
  identity, 134
  lobbyists, 147–48
  money and, 106–7, 124–27
  moving on up, 65–70
  power and, 151–74
  presidential, 181, 202–3
  unfairness of election process, xi,
    xiii–xvii
Porter, DuBose, 40–41
position vs. power, 161–65, 173
Posse Foundation, 180
possibilities, getting lost in, 5–7
poverty, xxi, xxii, 2, 9, 15, 16, 20, 22,
    23, 36, 56–58, 203
power, xiii, xv, xxvii, xxix, 4, 32, 36,
    72, 81, 151–74, 199–206
  beliefs and, 170–72
  challenging, 159–61
  changing the rules of
    engagement, 165–70
  fear and, 29–51

making what you have work,
    151–74
  mapping, 166–70, 173–74
  money and, 103–30
  opportunity and, 53–78
  position vs., 161–65, 173
  taking, 199–206
  taking stock and taking time,
    156–61
  winning and, 165–66
pre-K programs, 140
presidency, U.S., 181, 202–3
priorities, 183–86
prison, xv, xxix, 16, 179
privilege, 204–5
pro bono work, 87–88, 138, 164
property values, 104
Publishers Clearing House
    Sweepstakes, 103

QUEST (school program), 104
quotas, 62–64

race, xii, xiii, xiv, xvii, xx, xxi, xxiii,
    xxiv, xxvi, xxix, 4, 6, 15–21, 24,
    58–59, 76, 134, 136
  ambition and, 3–27
  discrimination, xxiii, xxvi, 15–22,
    40–48, 57–58, 61, 74–75, 106,
    116, 200
  failure and, 131–50
  fear and otherness, 29–51
  mentors and, 79–103
  money and, 103–30
  opportunity and, 53–78
  power and, 151–74
  Rodney King protests of 1992,
    15–20
  stereotypes, 9, 10, 41–48
  taking power, 199–206
  Work-Life Jenga and, 175–97
relationships:
  mentor, 79–103
  personal, 179–86, 192
relaxation, 193–95
religion, xxii, 31, 125, 134, 168, 169,
    176
reproductive choice, 156–57

Republican Governors Association, 203, 204
Republican Party, 40–43, 62, 136–37, 140, 141, 152–53, 156, 159, 169, 200, 202
retirement, 115
Rhodes Scholarship, xix–xxv, xxvii
risk, 141, 142, 148, 161
Roberts, Nora, xxvi, 89
Robinson, Ashley, 154–55
Rockefeller, John D., 11
romance novels, xxvi, 23, 88–89, 180, 182
Roseborough, Teresa Wynn, 24, 25, 87–88
rules of engagement, changing, 165–70

Sage Works, 163
same-sex marriage, 47
Saund, Dalip Singh, 24
scholarships, 104–5, 108, 109, 118, 140
science, xxiii–xxiv
secretaries, 68–70
Securities and Exchange Commission, 121
self-analysis, 201–2
self-care, 193–95
self-doubt, taming, 70–74
self-employment, 90–91, 111–12, 142–43, 158–59, 161–63, 186–87
  finances and, 111–17
self-help books, 154
sexual assault, 56
sexual orientation, 39, 46
  discrimination, 46–48
Shanaynay stereotype, 41, 43
Shark Tank, 125
side hustle, 114, 201
Silicon Valley, 60–61
singing, 131–33, 181
situational mentor, 85, 88–89, 101
slavery, 9, 24, 136
sleep deprivation, 186, 187, 189
social media, 56, 114, 146, 191, 205–6
soul, 22
South Carolina, 94
Spanx, 159

Spelman College, xxiii, 9–10, 11–14, 15, 16, 17, 21, 37, 79, 89, 93, 100, 105, 117–21, 189–90, 193–94
sponsor, 85–86, 101
sports, 56, 74, 177–78
staff meetings, 80–82
standardized tests, 140
Star Trek: The Next Generation, 166–67
start-ups, 34–35, 90–91, 142–43, 161, 162, 165
stereotypes, xxvii, 9, 32–33, 35, 39–48
  fear and, 32–48
  gender, 9, 10, 41–48
  race, 9, 10, 41–48
storytelling, xviii
Strike Team, 152–53, 158
success, xv, xxvii, 6, 55, 69, 71, 122
  fear of, 33, 35, 45–46
  self-made, 55–56
Sun Tzu, *The Art of War*, xvii
support staff, 68–70
Supreme Court, 181
Sutherland Asbill & Brennan, 138, 139
SWOT analysis, 65–66, 78

taking power, 199–206
taking stock and taking time, 156–61
taxes, 87, 107, 111, 112, 116, 138, 143–44, 145, 159
tech industry, 60–61, 106
television, 10, 17, 18–19, 37, 156, 166, 194
Telluride Association Summer Program, 7–9, 10, 20
termination of employees, 81–82, 139, 186–87
Texas, xxvi, 156
think big and act smart, 189–95
Thomas, Brian, 152, 158
time, prioritization of, 183–86
time, taking, 156–61
title loans, 114
titles, 155, 161–62, 173
triggers, 188
Trump, Donald, 202
trust, 192

truth, telling the, 143–45
Tubman, Harriet, 136
Tyson, Eric, *Personal Finance for Dummies*, 115

Uncle Tom stereotype, 43
University of Texas, xxvi
UPS, 139
urgency, 183–86

vacations, 193, 194
Vance, Lucy, 119, 120
volunteer work, xii, 62, 64, 67, 120, 138, 180
voter registration, 53–55, 169
voting discrepancies, xi, xiv–xv, xvii
voting rights, 16, 156

wanting more, 1–27
Washington, DC, 24
water, bottled, 142, 157, 165
Ways and Means Committee, 121
wealth, 12, 13, 21, 22, 55–56, 103–30
    gaps, 103–4, 106, 115–16
    See also money

Wells, Ida B., 58
White, Walter Francis, 16
Whole Foods, 142
Winfrey, Oprah, 159
winning, and power, 165–66
Wisconsin, 57
Women's National Basketball Association, 177–78
Work-Life Jenga, 175–97
    don't deal with jerks, 186–89
    first things first, 179–86, 196–97
    myth of balance, 175–76, 183
    prioritization, 183–86
    self-care and, 193–95
    think big and act smart, 189–95
writing, xxvi, 12, 13, 23, 88–89, 114, 157–58, 180, 181–83, 190, 191
wrong, best way to be, 145–48, 150

Yale Law Glee Club, 131–32
Yale Law School, xxvi, 38, 107, 108, 131–32, 181, 193
yoga, 194
youth vote, xiii